D0405061

MILLENNIUM

TOOLS FOR THE COMING CHANGES

by

LYSSA ROYAL

A Royal Priest Research Book

©1997 by Royal Research International
ISBN 0-9631320-3-2
Millennium: Tools for the Coming Changes
All Rights Reserved. No part of this book may be reproduced by any means
or in any form, except brief quotes for literary reviews, without written
permission from the publishers.

Published by:
Royal Priest Research Press
c/o PO Box 30973
Phoenix, Arizona 85046 U.S.A.

Cover Art:
Visionary Media
512-258-7311
Visionary1@earthlink.net
A graphic illustration and pre-press house with a flair for the cosmic.

First Printing, January 1998

Publisher's Cataloging-in-Publication
(Provided by Quality Books, Inc.)

Royal, Lyssa.
    Millennium : tools for the coming changes / by Lyssa Royal. —
1st ed.
    p. cm.
    "A Royal Priest research book."
    ISBN: 0-9631320-3-2

    1. Self-actualization (Psychology) 2. Visualization. 3.
Millennialism—Miscellanea. 4. Forecasting. I. Title.

BF637.S43.R69 1998   158.12
                                      QBI97-40971

Printed in the United States of America

TABLE OF CONTENTS

ACKNOWLEDGMENTS

In the fall of 1996 I was working on several books simultaneously, waiting for spirit to direct me toward the next book to be birthed. I sent an impassioned plea to the universe for guidance.

Because our previous book distributor went bankrupt, still owing us an embarrassing amount of money in back payments, I needed a compassionate investor. I also needed to know exactly which book should be published first.

Within an hour of making this passionate (and private) plea for guidance, I received an out-of-the-blue e-mail from a friend and supportive past client. It was as if he had heard my silent plea! He offered to finance this project, but he also told me exactly which book he envisioned needed to be published. Both of my requests were filled by the one I am simply calling my human angel. I call him **Q** for short. (He wishes to remain anonymous).

Q encouraged me to review my most profound material, have it transcribed, and send it to him for compilation. The format and structure of this book is primarily his. Once I received his first draft, I performed meticulous editing (for grammar and structure) and received even more material from the spirit realms to add to the volume. Without Q the book you hold in your hands would not have come to fruition. I am deeply grateful to him for holding this vision and lighting the fire under me to produce it.

Two individuals took on the tedious task of transcribing the channeled material from audio tapes. The first transcriber, **Sharon Jarrett,** had been offering her services for a year, but I had not been able to use her. Luckily, she was available to begin the project. After events in her life made finishing the project impossible, **Margot Reed** appeared (having been under my nose all along) to finish the task. To both of these wonderful women I send my heartfelt thanks.

Margaret Pinyan has edited all of my books since 1990. She is a brilliant woman with a razor-sharp mind. I shudder to think how mangled these words would be without her finesse, and the love and care she puts into each paragraph. I am eternally in her debt.

John and Denise Head of Visionary Media offered their professional services for the cover image, created from a photo I had taken at Chaco Canyon, New Mexico. Amidst their own blossoming business they put much love and effort into creating the image I wished to portray. First friends of my husband and now friends of mine, I cherish their addition to this project.

And finally, this project could not have been completed without the incredible unconditional love and support from my husband, **Ron Holt,** who has taught me the meaning of true love and the opening of the heart.

DEDICATION

This book is dedicated to our loved ones, those who cry and laugh with us and who wish the best for us even as we stumble in the darkness, confused by our own illusions. As we heal emotionally and spiritually, our relationships with our loved ones soar to new heights. This book is dedicated to those loved ones who have waited patiently for our growth so that new heights can be reached. As we reach these new heights, we see the divine reflected in the eyes of those we love. But first we have to see it within ourselves.

And personally, I dedicate this book to my loved one, my husband Ron, who has convinced me of the power of love.

PREFACE

In this chaotic and often confusing world we call Earth, our most important—and overlooked—resource is each other.

Since we as a species have been aware enough to ponder our place in the universe, we have received guidance from the unseen spiritual realms. This guidance might have come in the form of visions, speaking in trance, writing, artwork, or psychic intuition. Debating the reality of this guidance is futile; it appears in our world despite our disbelieving or cynical nature and becomes a dynamic force for transformation. Though this guidance might seem on the surface to give prophecy or cosmological information, the underlying intent of this spiritual assistance is to help us live more peacefully and joyously with each other—a skill we desperately need to master if we are to survive as a species.

The information presented in this book is a synthesis of over a decade of spiritual guidance given to me from these unseen realms by a myriad of loving spirit teachers who have pledged to assist humankind during this time of planetary transformation. In sharing this information it is their wish that the reader understand the purposes for the transmissions: to heal the human heart and assist humanity to build a global community of self-empowered beings who have mutual respect and love for each other and Mother Earth.

The guidance presented in these pages is available to all of us with the ears to hear it. I do not consider myself special in any way just because I have the skills necessary to bring these words to the reader. We all have the ability to interface with the spiritual realms, for it is one of our many birthrights as aspects of the universal source. One simply needs to commit oneself to developing the skill and to meet the trials and challenges inherent in the process.

It is my wish that you will read these words with an open heart and mind. May they help you value your life journey as a process of healing and growth rather than one of never-ending pain and challenge. Most of all, may these words help you value and honor your loved ones, who are your partners upon this journey. May you dissolve the barriers between you and walk the road to the divine together . . . for as we heal our relationships we in turn heal our planet and together enter a new era of human evolution.

— *Lyssa Royal*

THE SHIFT

There are many doorways through which the collective consciousness of a species may pass as it experiences its evolutionary journey. Some of these doorways manifest as agreed-upon symbols that are acknowledged by a culture.

Each new millennium triggers the opening of one of these doorways through the collective beliefs of a planetary civilization. The power is not in the counting of years based on a Gregorian calendar, but in a collective recognition of the milestone that a new millennium represents.

In this time upon the Earth when discontent is surging at the same rate as overwhelming optimism and hope, humankind holds a tremendous power in its hands—the power to create a planetary reality based on creative vision, blind optimism, and spiritual potential. The seeds of the future are held in human hands.

You as humans came into this life because you wanted to be here during one of the most exciting eras experienced by the people of your world. You are here to help create heaven on Earth. The population of the planet is so large today because so many souls want to be a part of Earth's transformation. These souls want to be a part of a shift in consciousness and heal themselves at the same time. All of these beings of light have chosen to play an enormous variety of challenging roles in order to help the whole of the planet grow.

The shift has begun, and it will be a catalyst for a tremendous transformation in human perception. Consciousness manifesting as a physical body has a natural evolutionary cycle. As each cycle comes to a close, a new cycle begins.

The current cycle (which is now coming to a close) can be referred to as third density, using a specific scale that measures the realms of existence. Density refers to a vibratory rate. The third-density rate is slower than the reality you are now entering, called fourth density.

Third-density reality is based upon the idea of separation. This means that you manifest your lives as separate from God, separate from yourselves, and separate from each other. In third density (or 3D) there is very little understanding of the concept of unity. This separateness is actually an illusion, but a necessary one for you to learn the lessons of third density. When these lessons are completed they will naturally move you from the third-density evolutionary cycle into fourth density.

In fourth density (4D) you have a higher frequency on the quantum level. You become less dense and radiate more light, literally and figuratively. You begin to express more of your natural state of existence, which is pure light. In fourth-density reality the illusion of separation ends and you begin to awaken to your natural state of integration or unity. You begin to realize that you are at one with the universe and one with the God Force. In 4D you begin to perceive that the universe is both outside you and within you, and that your external reality is just a projection of your internal one. You become conscious creator beings who recognize the links that exist between all of you as well as your inner connection to All That Is.

Frequency Bands of Consciousness

Densities describe the different states of existence experienced by consciousness as it journeys toward wholeness. A density is a frequency range of consciousness or a vibrational rate, much like a bandwidth on the radio such as AM, FM, or VHF.

Some individuals use the term "dimension" to denote the same idea, although to be technically correct, a dimension is something quite different. There are an infinite number of dimensions within each density. The densities, or frequency bands of consciousness, are defined as follows.

First Density: Atoms and Molecules
Awareness as a point; physical matter

This frequency level is the most basic. It provides the matter and energy for the creation of atoms and molecules. The basic life forms of mineral and water, for example, are all operating from a first-density orientation. You possess this frequency within yourselves as a foundation because it makes up the basic genetic codes and comprises the molecular level of the human body.

Second Density: Plants and Animals
Awareness as a line; development of group or species identity

The consciousness expressed by a second-density frequency does not possess the ego sense of self-awareness. Most species within the plant and animal kingdom exist here. However, their placement in dimensional reality and density depends upon many additional factors, including the presence or absence of ego. Currently, as humans are moving from third to fourth density, some species (such as certain primates) are moving from second to third density and displaying the rudimentary development of ego structures.

Third Density: Humans
Volumetric awareness; ego; linear perceptions of time; loss of group identity and development of individual identity; can remember the past and cognize the future while retaining present awareness

This is the density where human beings emerge. It is a vibration that creates the illusion of separation and thus a challenge toward awakening. Presently humanity is experiencing a transition period into fourth-density reality that can account for the many rapid changes and challenges the human race is now experiencing. Third density is the frequency that expresses the most separation from the whole. It is from here that many lessons about integration are learned.

Fourth Density: Metahumans, Pleiadians, and other 4D Civilizations
Superconsciousness; reintegration of group identity without loss of individual identity; cyclical and fluid perceptions of time; perception of multidimensional and multidensity realities; negatively oriented consciousness becomes more difficult to maintain

At the present time on Earth, fourth-density reality is overlapping third. The vibrational rate of reality is increased from 3D,

3

therefore one might be faced with personal issues in a much more intense way. As the self seeks the wholeness of the 4D reality, resolution of personal conflict and relationships must be achieved. This is the frequency where self-responsibility, personal sovereignty, and clarity in communication become essential. This is the last density in which physical bodies are used as vehicles for the expression of consciousness. Many civilizations choose to spend long periods of time within fourth density.

Fifth Density: Spirit Guides and Masters
Experiential awareness of "I" as a group identity; pure energy state; not bound by linear time

In this density, sentient consciousness begins to awaken to its heritage. This is the density of wisdom. Many from this realm choose to become nonphysical spirit guides to those in physical bodies. A fifth-density being merges with its family of consciousness or oversoul and begins to remember. This is the first density in which a nonphysical orientation is experienced.

Note: There is no clear-cut distinction when transitioning from fifth to sixth and from sixth to seventh densities. Because these densities are not physically oriented, there is much blending in these transitions.

Sixth Density: Star Trek's "Q" (a simplistic example)
A conscious frequency band unto itself might manifest as group consciousness or individualized personalities that express the basic qualities of limitlessness and unified consciousness

This has often been called the Christ consciousness density. It is a frequency level equal to the examples displayed by the Christ or Buddha. From this frequency a total remembrance occurs, and one begins taking responsibility for the whole rather than the self. The process of evolving the self and the whole becomes one and the same. The character known as Q from *Star Trek: The Next Generation* (without his tendency to cause trouble!) might suffice as an example of a sixth-density consciousness.

Seventh Density: A Holistic System of Consciousness
Awareness as the multidimensional experience
Analogy: a shattered mirror whose pieces have been reassembled into near-perfect condition, yet still remembers the experience of the past fragmentation

This is the frequency of total oneness or integration. Those who vibrate to this frequency are merged in identity and become a mass-consciousness whole. They serve as a magnet to those in other frequencies and provide the current for the natural flow toward integration. They lead the way to the next octave of experience.

Progression through the Density Bands

Existence is not just a linear progression through the various densities. You actually exist within all densities at the same time. Your soul can perceive this multidensity presence; your ego is not able to experience this perception. Your whole being projects simultaneously through all of the densities rather than experiences evolution in a step-by-step process.

This occurs because outside the human experience, time is not linear. All ideas and experiences occur simultaneously. You will not understand this concept through your intellect alone because intellect is based on ego knowledge, which is linear. You can understand it only through your inner, nonlinear senses. Try sensing through your heart that everything past, present and future is happening in the eternal now. Linear time is merely an invention that allows you the illusion of doing one thing after the other in sequence. Linear time also helps you experience the idea of separation and fragmentation that is essential to 3D learning.

As you project your consciousness through all of these densities simultaneously, you can connect with future selves, higher selves, and past lives. You are everything all at once. It is only the ego that needs the confines of linear reality to organize its experience. This is not a negative idea. It is simply a part of the physical 3D human experience. Let us illustrate with an example from computer technology. You have the ability to send simultaneous e-mails to a list of recipients. If you look at the sender of the e-mail as the oversoul and the recipients as the various fragmented parts of the self, you can see how an exchange of energy can occur simultaneously. It is the same idea. The only difference is that your oversoul's "recipients" might be in the "past" or the "future," which is not a limitation to the oversoul.

Let us use an example of a paddle and ball connected by a rubber band. When you hit the ball and it is the farthest away from you, the rubber band is stretched. That represents third density because you are at the farthest point of separation. When the ball returns to you, its momentum is created from the force of its separation. This is where you are now as a planet. You have been gathering momentum to sustain you through the far reaches of separation. As separation ends and you begin returning to the source, the ball appears to travel very quickly and with much force. You are seeing this now as you enter 4D and begin the integration process. This process is always cyclical.

First and second density—the beginning of the cycle—are actually much more integrated than third density. First density contains the consciousness that animates All That Is. These are the molecules and atoms that make up the rocks and basic building blocks of life. You have first density within you. Your first-density counterpart is in the atoms of your very being.

The primary idea of second density is that of an egoless state. There is no awareness of selfhood. When you progress to third density you attain an ego personality state. The human birth process goes through these three stages as well. When you are conceived in the womb, you are at the first-density level of consciousness. You are the cosmic "soup" of creation. When you are born, you are second density. You do not have an ego at that point, and you do not differentiate between yourself and your environment. As you grow, you develop an ego and achieve a third-density level of consciousness.

At this point in Earth history you are being presented with an option to progress to a fourth-density consciousness. This entails moving beyond the ego's individual ability to say "I am" and transition to a level of consciousness capable of expressing the state of "we are." This is a natural process of evolution and a hallmark of fourth density.

Mechanics of the Shift

Your transition into fourth density will not be like a flick of a light switch. It will be more gradual. To illustrate, let us say that you have water and air. The water is much warmer than the air,

6

thus they are vibrating at different frequencies. This produces a mist, which is a combination of the two.

These three realms—water, air, and mist—can be likened to 3D (water), 4D (air), and the transitional period (mist). At this moment you exist within the mist. You carry within you the characteristics of both 3D and 4D. It will be many years until you evolve from the mist state and exist totally within the air state. You will see such remarkable changes in your life within the next decade or two that it will seem as if you have entered a whole new reality.

The reason that the evolutionary process takes a period of time is because evolution does not just occur on the physical levels. It also must occur within your emotional, mental, and spiritual bodies as well. An evolution of consciousness is the essential ingredient in this shift.

Right now on Earth the frequency is shifting, but consciousness has not yet synchronized with the changes in frequency. It is a delicate process. When the progressions in consciousness frequency and Earth frequency are not synchronized, a form of friction can occur. This state of nonsynchronization (or disharmony) is temporary. Because consciousness is connected to your cellular structure, a commitment to its evolution virtually guarantees your physical evolution. It is just a matter of time.

The individuals who resist this change will experience discomfort, as in the following illustration: As you move through the mist, you become less dense and anything you are carrying within your being that is heavy (such as denial or unresolved issues) pulls you down. You will become more aware of these issues. As you become less dense, your darkness becomes more apparent and obvious. You must look at these aspects of the self rather than deny them, otherwise transformation becomes extremely difficult.

The ego often plays tricks to get you to ignore the darkness and not deal with it. One of these tricks is to get you to embrace the philosophy that you will be saved or rescued from this Earthly existence by extraterrestrials or by adherence to a certain religion. This is just another way for humanity to play out its denial of self-responsibility. You have all chosen to be here for personal and planetary reasons. Seeking to escape will not help you or your planet, but will only further separate you from the whole of yourself.

In the following chapters we will explore the transformational experience as humankind evolves from third density to fourth density and beyond. The mental, emotional, physical, and spiritual aspects of this evolution will be addressed and several exercises will be suggested to help create a smooth and effortless transition.

2

TRANSFORMATION AND OPPORTUNITY

The transformation discussed in the previous chapter has also been referred to by many teachers as an *ascension* process. Basically, this process is a shift from one reality to another.

You might have heard a version describing this process that says that during ascension your physical body will turn into light and vanish from the physical plane. Another version you may have heard is that you are going to become like Christ and experience a physical death and rebirth. Another version of the ascension is that you are going to be rescued by extraterrestrials and removed from this planet. In the more traditional biblical sense, the ascension is also known as the Rapture, which mean that you will simply vanish and reappear in the arms of Christ.

Think about those different scenarios deeply and feel them within you. Do they feel right to you? Do you think that everyone will have exactly the same experience?

In reality, no one will have an identical experience. Each of you will experience your own unique process of transmutation. Some of these processes might be dramatic, whereas others might be very subtle. If you judge your progress by the progress of another, then you will lose sight of the experience itself.

Think for a moment of the caterpillar. You are like a caterpillar right now. A caterpillar comes in many different colors. It has its own rich and beautiful experiences and might never dream that there is anything more to life. One day Ms. Caterpillar sees Mr. Caterpillar seemingly disappear. In reality this is just a misunderstood metamorphosis. She does not understand what he has experienced.

Mr. Caterpillar might return to Ms. Caterpillar in a butterfly form and try to communicate. If she recognizes him, Ms. Caterpillar might judge that he is crazy or might judge that he has had a spiritual revelation that she has not had, and therefore he is to be idolized. Your planet's transformation most likely will not be as visually evident as the difference between a caterpillar and a butterfly, but emotionally you will feel the same tremendous change.

When you start seeing another person go through the metamorphosis it means that you too are experiencing the same process. If you can see it in another person, you are experiencing it yourself. Look around at your friends and loved ones. Watch their metamorphoses. When you begin to see their changes, be assured that yours are occurring as well.

The caterpillar goes into a cocoon before its transformation and enters a deep sleep or period of stasis. During this quiet time the caterpillar has its own experiences that are a byproduct of the transmutation. The previously held reality of the caterpillar begins contracting and it feels a sense of isolation, as if the world is closing in around it. How many of you feel this even now?

Many people are feeling isolated and alone. Some are deliberately bringing this isolation into their lives by not watching television, not listening to the radio, not reading the newspapers, but instead keeping their focus on their spiritual path. That is an example of the human version of the caterpillar going into the cocoon to begin its metamorphosis.

As your reality starts temporarily contracting, you won't lose your memory of the greater whole, but you might experience a feeling of aloneness or separateness that will be different from anything you have ever felt before. If you feel that you want to isolate yourself or if you feel very alone even with friends all around you, do not fret. It is normal and natural. It is part of the cocooning stage.

When you build your cocoon, you energetically create around you an egg or shell of energy like a caterpillar does, but it is made of light fibers. This sheath covers you completely and protects you.

These light fibers charge the cellular energy in your body all the way down to the meta-atomic level (which is the level beyond the atomic level not yet visible with today's scientific instruments). The fibers charge you. They heal you. They provide a period of safety and healing for the body so it can begin its delicate transformation.

If you want to encourage the process, think about this cocoon of energy around you from time to time. Make it any color you wish. The colors might change according to your energy balance at any given moment. While you are in this cocoon, many changes will happen, but they will be different for each person.

The first shift will be in your emotional body. You will experience new and different emotions. You will also experience old emotions you thought you had already processed. If this happens, do not judge yourself. This is part of the healing process. Those who are involved in the alternative health field know that a healing crisis brings up symptomology, and those symptoms are a sign of actual healing.

When does this caterpillar emerge from its cocoon? Each of you has your own "birthday," which corresponds to your individual timing, but awakenings often happen in groups. The timings of these group awakenings are often determined by astrological alignments that reflect universal and archetypal principles. Those who are interested in astrology should note that the north and south nodes often reflect group awakening processes.

When the butterfly finally comes out of the cocoon, it awakens as if it's been in a deep sleep. It rubs its eyes. It stretches its new wings into the sunshine. Life as a caterpillar is a vague memory, almost like a dream. The butterfly thinks it has merely gone to sleep and then awakened. It does not realize that it was not always a butterfly.

This has a very specific translation for humans. You will not one day wake up and say, "I have ascended!" Instead, you might not necessarily notice that you have changed at all. You will have a feeling of continuity, as if you have been a butterfly all along. This allows for a smooth transition with little fear. It is not that you become something totally different. Instead, you become more of the potential that has always existed within you. The only difference is that now the potential becomes active. Your old, limited self becomes a dim memory that is gradually forgotten altogether.

The Darkness and the Light

You are going to metamorphosize. To bring it about, you will have to integrate yourself by befriending the darkness inside you more than ever before. Any denial of who you are, especially the darkness, will slow your metamorphosis. If that happens, it can become painful. You must seek to embrace the darkness, for without it you cannot ever truly embrace the light. (Embracing the darkness does *not* mean serving it. This will be explored in later chapters.)

There has been much talk about the antichrist in prophetic literature. Is he going to come? What is he? Is it one person? Is it an idea? The whole idea of the coming of the antichrist in an archetypal sense means the coming of your own darkness. Just as your own christhood is approaching, so is your own dark-ness—your own personal antichrist within you. It is only through the meeting of those two polarized energies within you that the metamorphosis can take place. It is just like mixing two chemicals together and waiting for a chemical reaction. You cannot have a reaction with only one chemical. The transformation is achieved through integrating the two. When you embrace both the light and the dark, it is then that you are able to transform.

How do you face your darkness? What do you do with your darkness? The only tool you have in the here and now (in a physical tangible sense) is your current physical life. It is impor-tant for you to journey deeply into your life, into the pain and the darkness. This does not mean that you have to rehash it, but you do need to *own* it.

Owning your life means that you will need to understand that you created it through your own choices. You are never a victim. Your responsibility in life is to choose to respond in a way that promotes your growth and healing. When you begin to unravel the threads of your life and examine them, feel them, and own them, you must recognize that you are at cause before you can evolve. At that point of realization, you begin facing your own darkness.

When you face the darkness it is a catalyst that begins the evolutionary process of metamorphosis like the caterpillar in the cocoon. You cannot do this simply on the mental level. It must be done on the emotional and spiritual levels as well. Your mental body cannot orchestrate this, because it is ruled by the ego. Instead of allowing you to approach the darkness the ego will do whatever it can to protect you from it by creating elaborate illusions to frighten you away from it.

There are many ways to explore the inner archetypal darkness. You can do this through the exploration of dream imagery. Shamanic activities such as drumming and ceremony or ritual bypass the mental body and affect deep aspects of the psyche. Shamanic ritual creates an experiential transformation and it is through this that darkness and light can converge. Transformation then begins. For thousands of years the native peoples of Earth have understood the power of darkness and light and have experienced the intensity of transformation created by the integration of those aspects. Today's western society has dispelled belief in the power of archetypal healing through ritual, judging it to be part of an ignorant, primitive age. However, the human psyche needs this type of healing on an ongoing basis. It is essential for the survival and evolution of the species.

It is not your responsibility to force humanity to change or process its darkness. That would be a distraction from your own individual healing. The only thing you can do as an individual is to be responsible for yourself, to act with integrity in all matters, and heal *yourself.* Therein lies one of the most significant services that you can provide for the planet as a whole.

Spread your light into the world with no strings attached. When you become too concerned with changing others, you can never truly change yourself. Transformation always begins within and then affects the world automatically.

Shift yourself, and the world around you responds.

Once you begin facing your darkness, it is like a snowball rolling down a hill. The process takes on a life of its own. Do not run from it. The only thing you have to do is simply be in the moment. Whenever dark memories from the past or new experiences in the present unfold before you, do not run. Confront them directly in the here and now. Allow the experiences to make you strong

13

through confrontation and transformation rather than avoid and resist them.

Anytime you resist your reality it as if you are saying to the universe, "I did not create this; get it away from me!" Since your creations literally *are* an aspect of you, you would be rejecting yourself.

You create everything that comes to you. When you send something back—like sending back cold soup in a restaurant that you own—you deny your own creation. When you deny your own creations, you deny yourself.

Each creation that births from you contains an opportunity. Embrace that opportunity no matter how dark it is, and remember that you must have had a good reason for creating it or it would never exist. There is always an intrinsic value to every experience, even the darkest, and the greatest masters of life learn how to grow from each and every one of those challenges.

The idea of mastery has been misunderstood. Many people have the perception that you come to Earth to be trained as masters. In reality, it is just the opposite. You are *already* masters when you come to Earth. The challenge is to use your mastery in this extremely confusing and disorienting third-density experience. Therefore, you are simply remembering your already-attained mastery and learning how to apply it in the challenging schoolhouse called Earth.

You have battled light and dark an infinite number of times and really do know how to integrate the two. The biggest challenge that you experience on Earth has to do with its distractions, a result of the chaos and confusion. You are distracted by what everyone else is doing instead of focusing on your own journey of empowerment. When you choose to judge others according to your own beliefs and expectations, tremendous distraction ensues.

If you allow yourself to be totally centered in your own mastery, you would not even look outside you or care what is happening. You would focus only on your own process of growth, knowing that it reflects the whole. Many individuals also assume that if they can learn tricks like levitation, teleportation, or spoon-bending, then their level of mastery increases. However, focusing on those external diversions to prove mastery is missing the point. A master is *not* one who performs feats. Feats are simply a natural byproduct of mastery and will come about when you remember who you are. The irony is that when you fully remember who you are, those feats no longer excite you!

PROCESSING DARKNESS
(Meditation Exercise)

This is a powerful exercise that will help you process some of your darkness. Get comfortable and use whatever technique you prefer that will take you into your quiet space.

Imagine that you are walking down a corridor into a room where there is a big mirror. Stand in front of the mirror and imagine that you see the most hideous version of yourself that you can picture. Make sure it is repulsive. For example, if you are concerned about being overweight, make your mirror image obese.

Reach your hand into the mirror and pull out the image of yourself. Connect your hearts together with a beam of green energy. Then embrace this image. As you embrace, feel love and compassion for this figure, who lives inside you and is very frightened. Allow that figure to merge with you energetically until you are one. Stand there embracing your merged self.

      ✧   ✧   ✧

This meditation is extremely powerful, because the more you do it, the more you process energy on an unconscious level. Do it as often as you can. The more you do it, the more you will notice your dreams changing. At first your dreams might seem darker and more intense, but as time goes on they will become more empowered. You will start processing much more rapidly in your dreams. This meditation conveys a symbolic message to your unconscious that says you now wish to embrace your totality and become a whole being, that you are now willing to love and accept your full self.

This process is not something you can do with your mind only. It must be done internally by using internal symbolic language that can reach your unconscious mind. You cannot relay messages to your unconscious by using the language of the intellect but only through the universal language of archetypal symbolism. The

15

exercises shared with you in this book will use such archetypal language.

In your world today darkness is being expressed through the various addictions and fears that plague society. It is important to see addictions as one externalization of the darkness, which in itself has a very positive interpretation. Instead of darkness being sequestered in the closets of the heart and mind, a healing crisis is being expressed. Addictions are one stage in a healing process, because the darkness is finally revealing itself.

The next step is the process of embracing the self, of owning the creations and moving forward. Many people in society are doing this by coming to terms with the pain in their childhood from familial alcoholism and/or sexual abuse. The darkness is emerging—*it must!* It must also be acknowledged. The longer it is denied, the more pain it will cause. These addictions are not a sign of your destruction, but a sign of your healing.

You are on the brink of a tremendous transformation. You are literally standing on the precipice ready to jump off the cliff, but you haven't convinced yourself that you have grown your butterfly wings. It was a long, hard climb up that hill, but you are standing at the edge of the cliff now waiting to jump. All of that hard work is behind you. You are tired, and you want to rest before you jump. However, you must gather the last bit of energy and jump, trusting your newfound wings. No one can stand behind you and push. You must take your own steps and make your own decisions in your own unique timing.

Hallmarks of Transformation

The transformation or ascension experience is a subjective one based upon individual perception. For instance, a subjective point of view simply means that the individual's perception of time and space begins to change, perhaps feeling less limited by time and space than before, thus perceiving new abilities previously ignored.

Always remember that reality cannot be separated from the observer. The observer and the observed are part of the same thing. In the overall scheme of things there is actually no such thing as objective reality! That is an illusion you have maintained

16

in third-density experience. Being a part of creation itself, you and the universe are ultimately one, which means that all experience is subjective. A true understanding of this concept is obtained when one transcends the ego and moves into a greater awareness.

One hallmark of the transition is that you will experience a new perception of the various connection points in time. Points in time will seem to be connected to other points in time in a more fluid way. Between those points it will look as if only a moment has passed.

Let's say that last Sunday you were visiting people you have not seen in a whole week. During the week you really missed them. During that week time seemed to stretch so very slowly. When the following Sunday came and you saw them again, those two points in time—the previous Sunday and the present Sunday—linked suddenly as if they were consecutive events. It might then have seemed as though no time at all had passed.

The illusion on the part of the perceiver is that she has transcended time and space and leapt from one point in time to another, even though she had lived a whole week in between. This is a phenomenon that you will experience more and more in the coming years. It is a perceptual change rather than a mechanical one. A scientist with an objective view of reality might attribute this to a mechanical change when it is truly just a perceptual one. If you look for a mechanical description of what will happen during the transformation, it would be inaccurate because mechanics are a byproduct of perception. That is an important thing to recognize. The outer reality is *always* a reflection of the inner one.

In fourth density there are gradients. Right now you have a foot in 4D and a foot in 3D, so to speak. In early 4D the idea of transcending time and space for space travel, for example, is not applicable. However, the deeper you move into 4D, the more you disengage yourself from 3D and the more possible it becomes. At that point your scientists will no longer be scientists as you have known them for the last five centuries. These scientists, no longer focused on the mechanical, will become philosopher-scientists once again as they were in the earlier days.

When these new philosopher-scientists discover how to master hyperspace travel, it will be an instantaneous "aha!" The concept of reality will be understood. It will not require months of research

17

and development because it will not be focused on the mechanical. This full realization will not be achieved until you evolve more deeply into 4D, but you will soon be approaching those philosophical changes in consciousness that will lay the foundation of a tremendous paradigm shift.

Your awakening will first require an *awareness of awareness* that goes beyond the intellectual. Most people in your world are not really aware that they are aware. They are not aware of their own consciousness. The first step on a more massive scale would be for people become aware of their own consciousness in a way that surpasses a simple theoretical or intellectual understanding. This awareness must become so real that it becomes the underlying driving force of your collective existence. The result of such a shift in self-awareness will trigger a deep change of perception on a mass level. As this happens, the world as you know it will shift dramatically, reflecting a new paradigm of higher awareness and conscious evolution.

3

CONSCIOUS EVOLUTION

In fourth density you will begin experiencing new and different perceptions in your life and in your consciousness. Think of the current shift in consciousness as a wake-up call. You finally realize that the alarm clock has been ringing. You have been hitting the snooze button for a very long time, but you can do that no longer. You *must* awaken to the greater reality.

The following exercise is very simple, and it provides a metaphor to explain the awakening experience.

AWAKENING THE SELF
(Meditation Exercise)

Put yourself in a comfortable position, eyes open or closed. Breathe deeply. Listen to the silence around you. Stretch your perceptual abilities and listen to the sounds that you normally filter from your awareness.

Listen to the clock ticking, the birds singing, or the hum of electrical appliances. Pay direct attention to these sounds and acknowledge their reality. If you smell something, pay attention to it. If you see anything with your inner vision such as colors or pictures, pay attention to those perceptions. If you feel anything on your skin, pay attention to it. Stretch your perceptive abilities and peer into realms that you usually ignore. Take at least fifteen minutes to complete this exercise. If you practice this exercise frequently, you will begin to expand your perceptions beyond your previous capabilities. A new world will open for you.

☼   ☼   ☼

Recognize that you are continually bombarded with stimuli, including stimuli on the more esoteric and energetic levels. If you can begin using this exercise to help you learn to perceive subtle stimuli, it will be a stepping stone toward your ability to perceive even more subtle energy from other levels of reality.

When doing this exercise, you enter a new world inside your consciousness. You go within and expand yourself outward in order to perceive a new dimension of the universe that you normally filter from conscious awareness. This is what will be required of you as you move into the fourth-density reality. You must begin to expand your perceptions in such a way that you no longer ignore the things that went unnoticed in the past.

As you move more into fourth density, you hold more light. You begin joining with the Creator, with each other and with more of yourself. This will require that you begin paying attention to the information and guidance coming to you from subtle levels of the universe and from deep within yourself.

You will begin having more profound dreams. You will have more insight, more psychic ability and precognition. You will be able to sense energy fields in a different way than in the past and you will be able to understand your inner world in a whole new way. With your loved ones you will have a deeper empathic connection. Prepare yourself for this. Know that you will never receive information or experience changes for which you are not ready.

It is going to become more and more important that you take quiet reflective time for yourself, even if it is only while driving down the road or doing the dishes. During that quiet time practice the awakening exercise and listen to that which is around you on the subtler levels. You will become a more finely tuned antenna through which you will perceive new and wonderful realities. Your clarity as a receiver will increase as a byproduct of this exercise.

Some people would deny this aspect of themselves. They retain a rigid view of reality, unwilling to expand their perceptions. Those people might have a difficult time during this transformational shift because friction will occur in their consciousness. As it does so, it brings up a lot of painful emotions. So it would be helpful to share this information with your loved ones in whatever way they can understand it. Encourage them to open and expand their perceptions of the universe so that as this change occurs, they can flow with it rather than be frightened by it.

Communicating with Extraterrestrial Cultures

As a planet completes its third-density cycle and begins its move into fourth density, the inhabitants must begin to face the reality of other life forms in the universe. This is where you stand now. These other life forms might exist in a nonphysical state, in multidimensional realities, or might come to your planet physically. They might meet with you openly when there is a sufficient common ground upon which contact can be based. Because your planet is not yet ready for widespread open contact with extraterrestrials, these other life forms will communicate with you through the only means open to them. Right now that means targeting receptive individuals through dreams and meditations as well as through telepathic contact such as channeling.

Humans are connected to many extraterrestrial life forms genetically and spiritually. Beings from the Pleiades, as an example, share the same extraterrestrial forefathers as Earth humans. You have been told that you have evolved from apes. However, in reality, if evolution on Earth had occurred naturally and without outside interference, it would have taken far longer for humanity to evolve to where it is today.

There has been intervention in human evolution in many forms by physical and nonphysical extraterrestrial beings throughout time. These beings have helped to guide the development of *Homo sapiens* as it grew and evolved. Humanity's off-plant forefathers have been watching Earth with great interest for quite some time. It is hoped that Earth will obtain a state of consciousness that represents a global unity whereby it would then meet its galactic family and connect with them face to face to begin the next natural phase of planetary evolution. [See the books *The Prism of Lyra* and *Preparing for Contact* by Lyssa Royal for more information on these ideas.]

21

All beings of a fourth-density nature have a need to seek out others and connect. The need to connect is a driving force in fourth density. In third density, on the other hand, the driving force is separation. This has created a militaristic, warring mindset that does not represent who you truly are. It is simply an expression of your fear, which must be explored in third density. Nothing has ever been "wrong" with third-density experiences, because those are the inherent lessons of 3D life that every society must learn.

Many people are already feeling the changes caused by the shift. In the meditations and prayers of many (and in your heart of hearts) there is a longing to build more of a community. The desire might manifest as the wish to build a global community or one in your town or neighborhood. This is a direct indication that you are entering fourth density and beginning to integrate instead of fragment. There will be some pioneers who will lead the way toward a global community, and the rest of you who wish it will eventually follow.

As you move into fourth density, the vibrations change and your reality will begin to approach the limitlessness of the higher dimensions. It will then become easier for off-planet beings to interact with you in your reality. As you continue to transform, you are going to find more and more cases of actual face-to-face contact, though it will be some time yet before it occurs in a massive, widespread way.

One of the key factors that dictates which type of reality you experience (both collectively and individually) is your brain-wave frequency. Humans generate a collective brain-wave frequency, which then creates and solidifies the surrounding reality based on a set of paradigms that directly reflect brain-wave frequency and states of consciousness. Extraterrestrial beings emit different frequencies through which they too create the reality in which they find themselves.

Frequently human and ET brain-wave frequency realities are not compatible, thus preventing face-to-face contact. As your frequency shifts and you become more perceptive of the greater reality around you, you then become able to interface with other levels of reality. As the human consciousness evolves, so does the ability to generate more flexible and expansive brain states.

At this time there are isolated pockets of humans who are accelerating their movement into fourth density. These people are opening their perceptions, connecting with new levels of reality, and beginning to experience unconditional, universal love. There are also some who resist the flow of these changes, thus experiencing a lot of craziness in their internal and external worlds that often manifests as violence and fear. This accentuates the polarity of current life on Earth and the need to choose a progressive and healthy paradigm through which human evolution can be expressed.

At some point those who are resisting this change will become overwhelmed. If they choose not to transform during this life, they may kill each other off, die a natural death at the end of their life span, or perish in natural disasters. They might then choose to come back to Earth in 4D or reincarnate into another 3D reality to continue their unfinished lessons. It is really up to the individual soul to choose how he wishes to make the transition. It is all up to each of you individually. There is no punishment for a refusal to transform. This eventually leads to greater understanding of the self and the universe. For those wishing to continue their evolution in 3D reality, more life experience is made available on various levels of reality.

Three hundred years into your future you will have long acknowledged the existence of extraterrestrial beings. Some of them will be living openly with you on Earth. You will have opened yourselves galactically and unified globally. This is a nexus point in your history-to-be. Even though there are always probable realities, there are nexus points in time/space around which many events revolve. The time period of the last decade of the 1990s and the first decade of the 2000s is a major nexus point that will dictate the probable reality you choose for your future.

You cannot wait for another to heal your world; you must each take responsibility. There are an infinite number of choices leading to an infinite number of possibilities for your future. The important thing is to make your choices wisely *now*. The actions that you take from these choices will shape your future in a profound way.

Your choices dictate your frequency, and your frequency dictates your reality.

Reality is never objective. It is always subjective because you are the creator of it. If there are ten people in the room with you right now, then there are ten realities superimposed over each other. You are all interacting within your overlapping realities based on your perceptions and beliefs. There is a general consensus reality composed of the compatible paradigms of each of the ten people in the room. If you want to change your individual reality, that entails changing your thoughts and beliefs. If you want to change your consensus reality, that entails changing the overlapping paradigms themselves. This comes from first changing individual thought. It all comes back to personal responsibility.

The Flatlander Paradigm

Familiar to many, the Flatlander story illustrates the challenge people have in conceiving of a fourth-density reality. Imagine a flat sheet of paper representing a two-dimensional world. Beings on that world can comprehend width, but not height. Width is their reality paradigm. One day a sphere comes wandering into the space occupied by Flatland, approaching from above.

Since the Flatlanders cannot comprehend height, they cannot see the sphere in its true form. Instead, as the sphere first contacts with the flatland reality, it appears as an inexplicable point stretching into a flat circle as it passes through Flatland, finally shrinking into a point and disappearing. The Flatlanders theorize madly about that strange point and flat circle, but they never discover the truth because they do not possess the ability to reach beyond the accepted paradigm.

Fourth density, as viewed from third, is just like trying to imagine the sphere from the limited perspective of the Flatlanders. The limitations of your reality (expressed by logical and linear thought) create necessarily incomplete views of the greater reality. Humans have a tool that can traverse all realms of consciousness so change can be sensed and understood on deeper levels, beyond the conscious. That tool is the imagination. For a very long time Western society has invalidated the imagination as a useless or even bothersome human frivolity. In actuality, without your imagination a smooth evolution would be almost impossible.

Whatever can be conceived through the imagination can be created in physical reality. You are limited only by the restrictions you place upon the tool of your imagination!

4

REAWAKENING COSMIC MEMORY

Imagine what it was like before you were born, as a soul contemplating life on Earth. Imagine the brilliance of your soul as it blended with your higher self and all the portions of you. Imagine what it was like at that moment—the excitement that your soul felt as it was getting ready for a grand adventure on Earth. Feel the power of the Creator in the light that you were emanating. Remember that you, as a manifestation of this light, can do anything.

From the perspective of that reality, nothing was impossible. You were a master of manifestation, of abundance, of joy and love. As this master you were choosing to have a life on Earth. In the light that you really are, you are tremendously creative. You can easily love and be loved. You have the ability to laugh, to share. Your nature is to move forward and grow in an endless cycle. You had all of these abilities when you chose to incarnate on Earth. These abilities are still a part of who you are.

Ponder this concept using the eyes of both your spirit and your physical body. Think for a moment of a glass of water, and let's say that the water represents spirit. Place that glass of water in a freezer and watch how, over time, the water freezes into ice. That ice is still water; it is still spirit. It is denser than the spirit that you once knew, but it is still spirit.

Your very bodies that you call home now are like that ice. Your bodies are *crystallized spirit*. Your spirit is not *in* your body; you *are* your spirit. The translation of your spirit in physical reality is a physical body, just as the translation of water in a cold environment is ice. It is the same idea.

27

As you interact with the world using your physical body (a crystallized spirit), you naturally utilize the talents and abilities that you have as a spirit. You naturally evolve and grow. Symbolically you have feet (which are also crystallized spirit) to move you through your reality and help you grow upon your path.

Your spirit also has the ability to express creativity as an extension of the Creator. As crystallized spirit you have hands with which to create in this physical world. As a spirit you have the ability for laughter, for love. As crystallized spirit you have a heart with which to express that laughter and love. You have a smile. You have sparkling eyes. These are all aspects of a crystallized spirit. They are gifts you have been given to express the natural spirit entity that you are.

This is why action and movement are so important in a physical world such as yours. In a nonphysical reality spirit can express itself by simply being. In a physical reality (as crystallized spirit) you must express your spirit through action by using the tools of your hands and feet, your heart and smile, and the light in your eyes.

At times individuals find it difficult to adapt to being crystallized spirit on Earth, but the gifts you have been given to help you adapt are plentiful. You, as crystallized spirit, have all the same abilities as your lightbody counterpart—the ability to create and affect reality thoroughly and effectively as a reflection of who you are.

Think of yourself as crystallized spirit so that you will feel your reality differently. Feel crystallized spirit within you, and as you do you will not feel a boundary between physical reality and your spirit. This is the secret contained within many of the native teachings of your world. These native teachers do not perceive boundaries between their spirit and the world around them. If you can practice this feeling even for one minute a day, it will lead you with ease to become able to do it for ten minutes a day once you establish the habit. That habit will eventually help enable you to walk around in your reality as a living, breathing, conscious crystallized spirit who is able to live life effortlessly.

Most people have known intuitively that the 1990s and just beyond were going to be the time of transformation. Many who have been involved in metaphysical or mystical thought for some time have known that they have been preparing themselves for this period of time. Until the end of the millennium (and into the new one) you might feel that your spirit is being tested. It is important to know that the only one doing any testing is yourself, and that you as a crystallized spirit would not be here if you did not have the ability to transform the planet into everything you envision it can be.

You are going to find that you will have a very intense focus in your consciousness, more so than you have ever had before. You will be able to accomplish things faster and more completely than you ever have before—as long as you are working in the flow rather than resisting it.

Those of you who have books you want to write or songs you want to sing must understand that *now* is the time to accomplish these desires. You will find that the reality around you will support you as long as you allow yourself to move with the flow.

On the other hand, what you resist will haunt you. Resistance is the denial of spirit. When you deny the flow, you resist the tide of evolution. Energy then builds up and what you resist will never go away. If you find tension, difficulty or frustration in one particular area of your life, ask in your prayers or meditations for the reason to be revealed.

Resistance will be more painful than ever before because of the acceleration occurring on the planet. The acceleration is like a snowball rolling down a hill. You will continue to gain momentum. It can be an exciting and wonderful time or, because of your resistance, a nightmare.

Many of you are concerned because you often seem to swing from a state of heightened consciousness back to a more mundane reality. This occurs partly because of the polarized nature of the reality in which you live. When people experience one extreme, they often unconsciously try to experience its opposite in order to balance it. This is not necessarily a conscious intention, nor is it something that will continue as you evolve. When you experience swinging back and forth, you can consciously stop at any moment and choose to take yourself to your center.

For instance, let's say that your meditation takes you to a high, then you come back down and feel very dense. When you start

29

feeling that denseness, close your eyes for a moment and take some breaths. Take yourself back through the beginning portion of the heightened experience you just had, but stop yourself at a center point rather than go higher.

Your desire might be to keep going higher and higher because the nature of your reality is to swing between polarities. Instead, take yourself only to what you perceive to be the center point between polarities, then open your eyes and go about your reality. If you find yourself experiencing the swing of a high and cannot seem to focus in this reality, then close your eyes and take yourself, through creative visualization, down through a level of separation. Seek to integrate spirit and matter. Go to the center point and stay there. If you train yourself to do this, you will begin to feel intuitively where that center point is so that you will not swing back and forth so easily.

At this time many people are craving simplicity in their lives. Those of you who want to simplify will find it easier to create your own realities. Those who are lost in their own chaos will create more chaos. Therefore, it is important to begin understanding what you need and want and take action. As you move through the doorway of fourth density, the dramatic energy shift on your planet will affect everyone as individuals.

There is no more time to wait. You must now begin *doing*— living your dreams, creating your excitement and letting go of anything that no longer serves you. Otherwise it will be a tremendous burden to you.

Simplification is also a good thing in terms of your societal systems. Right now certain systems in your society are very strained, such as the food system. One hundred years ago most of you were either self-sufficient or were in a community that could basically support itself. Now that you have centralized food distribution, in the event of a major crisis that distribution chain might be broken, causing tremendous disruption because most people have lost the knowledge to be self-sufficient.

It will benefit all of you to simplify your life by allowing yourself to be more and more self-reliant. In doing so you take the strain off the system so that it can expand and grow. A system can collapse when too many people become dependent upon it.

Your overall journey through physicality is ongoing. It seems slow only from the physical point of view. From the cosmic viewpoint it is more like the blink of an eye. Whenever you focus too much on plotting your way to the goal rather than enjoying the journey, the journey appears to take forever. When you consider everything else going on in the universe, the process you are now experiencing of integrating the dark and the light is considered by many galactic beings to be quite a lot of fun!

To use a dramatic analogy, what if you woke up in the middle of the night hanging upside down, the blood rushing to your head, something pressing on your chest, and you heard screaming? You would think, "Oh my goodness, something horrible is happening! I've got to get out of here!" Instead, imagine that you are in an amusement park on one of those rides that hang upside down; there is pressure on your chest and everyone is screaming all around you. Suddenly you remember that you are on a ride that you have chosen to experience. Yes, you are screaming your lungs out too, but you are having a great time doing it! It's all a matter of perspective.

When you "woke up" after being born in physical reality, you didn't understand the surroundings and you didn't take responsibility for being here. But when you decide to go to the amusement park and find yourself hanging upside down on the ride, you have full memory of why you are there. The horrible sensations you feel are even part of the fun.

In this life you are striving to regain your cosmic memory. When you regain that memory, time and space will take on a different meaning and you will not experience suddenly waking up hanging upside down on the roller coaster. The quality of the ride and what you make of it then become of paramount importance.

Empathy and Telepathy

Humans are naturally telepathic, but you have convinced yourselves that you are not. You will find that telepathic contact with each other (and your empathic abilities in general) will increase tremendously. This is a byproduct of the acceleration of frequency to which you are exposed as well as your own personal growth efforts.

Telepathy and empathic skills are a quality of fourth-density reality. Have you noticed how much more in tune you have been with other people? Are you finding that sometimes you even take on the emotions of others? The next challenge as you move into fourth density is to learn to tell the difference between your emotions and those of your neighbor.

With your increased sensitivity you will need to discern which emotions are yours and which are your neighbor's. Because of personal filters, issues, and illusions, it might be very difficult to know on the surface whose emotions belong to whom. Because of this, the following is recommended.

Let's say that you are a therapist and have a client who is very angry at her father. She spends an entire session processing this anger. When the session is over you suddenly find yourself very irritable, and at home you yell at your father. This means that you have taken on your client's energy. Simply sitting down and saying, "This is not me, it is my client's anger," most likely will not solve the problem by itself. Instead, you must automatically assume that when you feel an emotion—whether it is yours or not—that there is something within *you* that was triggered. If you are reacting, then an unresolved issue is signaling for your attention.

This does not necessarily mean that you are angry at your father. It might mean that the client triggered your anger at your own masculine energy, or your anger at your own authoritative self or inner parental archetype or something of that nature. Do not ignore the emotion and do not attribute it to the client and simply walk away. Since you feel it, you must own it, because it would not have manifested through you if you did not need to process it. You do not need to understand it, but you do need to *feel* it, process it, and release it.

When you can understand how you all trigger growth and evolution in each other through your emotional challenges, you will learn how to separate yourself from the emotions of your neighbor. When you recognize that your client or neighbor has triggered something in you, then you can move through it very quickly, no longer carrying the energy like a burden. In this way you can remain emotionally clear.

Aspects of the Transformation

Imagine that you are walking across a room that represents third density. You see a door and open it. You then walk into another room that represents fourth density. There are unfamiliar things on the walls, but it is an interesting place. You might feel differently about yourself here because the decor is more harmonious and more enriching to the soul. However, as you spend more time in this room you begin to realize that the walls are covered with mirrors. What you reflect is what you receive: If you let your inner beauty shine and express yourself through truth, honesty, and unconditional love, then the room will be a pleasant place. If you have not processed your emotions but instead continue to express yourself through fear, manipulation, secrecy and control, then you will begin to see an unbearable ugliness that will force a retreat back into the 3D room where you can hide from your reflections more effectively.

This is what the reality shift looks like, and you are already experiencing this on a daily basis. Many of you get a glimpse of your own beauty and power (4D), which terrifies you so much that you retreat into the safety of your judgments in 3D. You are learning to spend more and more time in that 4D room. At some point you will gather enough critical-mass energy that you will live permanently in the 4D room.

Humans often ask how they will know when they have moved into fourth density. It is not like a light being turned on and off. The definitions are not very clear to the ego. However, one clear way to know how much time you are spending in 4D is by evaluating how much time you spend in fear, judgment, and separation. The 4D room requires that you no longer be fooled by your own illusions. This might be harder than you realize.

You can begin to sense the change because you will feel differently. You might begin reacting differently to old stimuli. No longer will you become upset at things that used to upset you, for example. You can tell if you have shifted by how you react to the reality around you. Other than that, the signs can be quite subtle.

Each shift you make is like climbing a set of stairs. You are rising to new levels. The shift predicted by the Mayan civilization for the year 2012 will be like reaching a landing on the stairs before you start up another flight. The steps are taken at your individual pace, but the flow or momentum up the stairs is created by the mass consciousness.

It is as if you are all climbing steps in single file. It is okay to rest and let another person pass. However, you will not be able to take up a lot of space or keep people from continuing the climb because the momentum of the mass consciousness will be constantly pushing all of you up those stairs. The year 2012, for instance, represents the huge achievement of a large number of people arriving at the landing. At that point you will all hold hands (metaphorically speaking) and plan your strategy for the next journey up a new set of stairs.

Brain function will reflect the most obvious physical change due to the shift, opening doors for all the other changes your body will experience. There will also be changes on the genetic DNA level. You have been operating with a very small percentage of your genetic capability. Your species memory is still locked in a vault inside your genetics. These memories concern the origins of your species and your early days of interaction with your extraterrestrial forefathers.

This memory loss has kept the human race perpetually feeling like orphans. As the genetic changes begin, your memory will return little by little. It might feel like a shock wave that goes through your entire being, affecting every center of your body. When humanity regains full conscious memory of its heritage, it will literally become a different species that can then be called *metahuman*.

Transforming from Linear to Experiential Time

In third density you have learned to view time as linear. You perceive a sequential movement of time based on the external reality around you. You count time by the cycles of the moon and the sun—external manifestations.

When a civilization begins moving out into space and away from the influence of the solar system and sun, the question then becomes "How is time measured?" Do you create artificial time on a spaceship to model that of the system from which you have come?

34

What if the crew members come from many different worlds? This is not a problem you need to solve right now. However, it is on the horizon. The idea of experiential time (rather than objective time) will become more important as you move further into fourth density. Your perceptions of time will have changed and might be confusing to those who are unprepared.

Experiential time can be defined as an understanding of the movement of experience through the time continuum. Time will become based on internal experience rather than external manifestations. In third-density reality time can be likened to a straight line representing past, present and future. When you stand on this line and look down at your feet, all you can see is the line. All you see is past, present and future, which is an expression of linearity.

Imagine that you are a bird standing on a straight line that represents linear time in 3D. You decide to take wing, then fly higher and higher. When you fly high above the line you see that it is not a straight line, but it is actually curved. The higher you fly, the easier it is to see the curvature of the line. You were too close to the line earlier; you could see only a small part, which made it appear straight. As you rise above the line you see that it is curved. Your entire perspective has changed.

This is an analogy for what will happen in fourth density. You will rise above the line and your perception of time will thus move beyond that of past, present and future. You will see that all three exist simultaneously. You will begin to experience multidimensional thought even more than you have previously. This process has already begun.

In third density your vision is limited by linearity. In fourth-density reality time is viewed as circular or spherical, so there is never really a beginning or an end, simply a cycle (like the seasons). The 4D reality structure is so different that once born and raised in a 4D society with this model of reality, multidimensional awareness is easily achieved. Everyone is experiencing these changes. Your brains and conceptual abilities are changing. It will not be long before humans on a mass level begin expressing reality through curvature rather than linearity.

The perception of reality as cyclical has been held by native peoples of Earth since before recorded history. As Western society began its technological age, the belief in a linear reality has been a temporary distraction. Because Western beliefs have dominated planetary thought, many of Earth's ancient spiritual cultures have had to quietly hold the knowledge of a cyclical universe until humankind as a whole could remember its origins. As memory begins to return, the planetary paradigm will shift again into a more limitless view of reality and the universe.

Let us say that humans achieve space travel. As you develop your sense of experiential time, you will begin to move with the flow of universal synchronicity. This is truly a new perception of time based on experience and the rapidly changing frequencies of Earth. All 4D galactic societies experience time in this fashion. Since your perceptions have just begun to alter, it might seem a bit strange at first. You will need to disengage your linear, ego-based logical mind and learn instead to experience time through the soul.

Since all experience flows to the rhythm of the cosmic heartbeat (a universal frequency based on the golden mean spiral), one's species will not matter. The cosmic heart will keep time, and this timekeeping is expressed through the laws of synchronicity. This means that all beings will eventually unify and synchronize themselves through the higher frequencies of the heart.

The universal love frequency is expressed through the heart by the golden mean spiral and is a very real frequency measurable through machines available today. This frequency corresponds to the universal language of geometry. Geometry is expressed throughout all of creation in a unified field. As you transcend the physical realms and relearn this old language, time is replaced by experience, and experience shapes your sense of time into a sense of being. At this point all that exists is choreographed into an amazing dance that is perfectly timed and synchronous. This dance existed all along, but at this point you finally have the eyes to see it.

SENSING EXPERIENTIAL TIME
(Exercise)

To begin developing your sense of experiential time, the following exercise is recommended.

When you are driving in the car trying to get to your destination, imagine a piece of well-chewed gum. Mentally attach one end of the gum to your heart and one to your destination. Feel your connection to your destination through your heart. Relax and feel the fluidity of time and space. *Feel the experience of traveling to your destination to be as important as your arrival.* This travel time is important. Without it you would never arrive. Your travel time is another opportunity to experience consciousness.

☼   ☼   ☼

This exercise shows you that you are never separate from your destination. There is an energy that connects you to all things. When you focus on your movement through this energy—represented by your journey—you never have a sense of wasted moments. As you become more adept at this, you will develop a keen sense of timing so that even if you are late, the person you are meeting will also be late. If you are both late and arrive together, is that not arriving on time?

Now Is All There Is

You are in the process of rearranging the old belief that time is an endless march down a line and where step two is a sequential result of step one. You are learning to recognize that your power lies in the present moment and that the past and future exist simultaneously.

Just as the past and future influence your present, so also does the present influence the past and the future. Your power lies in the now through your present choices and actions. Your actions in the present rewrite your past as well as your future every moment that you exist.

You have believed that you drag around one fixed past like a suitcase that gets heavier each day. This is a result of living in the paradigm of linear time, which is really just an illusion to be used as a convenience in 3D reality.

From your natural state of existence as a soul there are no time constraints, only experience. As a soul you see the whole picture and know that you have the ability to live simultaneously in all probabilities. The past to which you are attached exists for a reason. Once you remember and embrace the concept that your past can be used as a teacher, you then release its anchoring effect and bring all of its energy into the here and now. It then becomes part of your present. Healing can occur only in the present because the present is the true point of power.

5

KEYS TO PHYSICAL TRANSFORMATION

Human physical bodies have existed in a third-density reality for many thousands of years. You are operating with a specific biochemical and genetic coding in 3D. This coding was shaped by the underlying template of your creation as a species. It represents what your entire species and your individual souls wish to learn—the integration and mastering of polarity.

The ultimate expression of polarity is the illusion that you are separate from the All That Is. This has been your challenge for the past several thousand years. You are now learning how to live with this illusion of separation and recognize your connectedness to All That Is so you can move from separation to integration.

As you move into 4D, illusion begins falling away and the conscious understanding of the human potential and your divine connection comes to the forefront. This new paradigm of thought requires actual changes to take place in the physical body. These changes will be triggered by the increased energy to which you will be exposed.

The Electric Body

As a transducer of electricity, you will be channeling this increased energy through your body and your consciousness. Since you need to learn to channel more energy through you, your body must adapt. This adaptation will occur naturally even if you take no steps to assist the process. However, if you do not assist the process it could take longer or cause discomfort for some of you. As time goes on, you will learn to recognize the symptomology of the shift and take control of the situation rather than become discouraged by it

Your bodies are conductors of electricity and you are bioelectric in nature. You are more than 90 percent water. As your voltage increases, you will need to conduct electricity and cosmic energy in a different and more efficient way than ever before.

Water

Since your bodies contain such a high percentage of water, it will be the single most important element during this time. The importance of drinking a lot of water needs to be emphasized. Purified water (not plain, untreated tap water) would be most beneficial. Tap water contains substances that increase toxicity. Drink at least 8 to 12 glasses of water per day, or as much as you feel your body needs to clear yourself of toxins. Also remember to eat foods that have a high water content, such as fruits and vegetables.

Allow yourself to *feel* fluid. This might sound rather abstract, but when you are feeling fatigued or raw emotionally, imagine yourself as a river current. The more you can imagine yourself fluidly moving like water, the easier you will adjust to the electrical changes that both your body and the planet are experiencing. Water will clear your electromagnetic field. When ingested, it helps release toxins in your body. When you bathe or shower in it, emotional toxins are released. This helps to keep you clear and balanced.

If you live near an ocean or lake, you have a wonderful opportunity to be near water. If you live in the desert it would be helpful to create a water environment in your home. For instance, you might want to get a fish tank and fill it with rocks and water so it resembles a pond. Sit peacefully and watch, feel, smell, and sense the water. Put a variety of rocks and crystals into it. Having water around your auric field will be very beneficial as your body begins to adjust to the frequency shift. Be creative! Use your bath or Jacuzzi to soak your feet every day. You will notice a difference in the way the electromagnetic energy is conducted around your body. If you feel fragile, it will help smooth and balance you.

Earth

The element of earth is also extremely important as you learn to conduct more electrical energy. Many of you already know the trick of putting your bare feet on the Earth when you feel a bit spacy and ungrounded. Simply put, the Earth absorbs the excess energy you discharge. It helps balance you. You might want to increase your contact with the Earth through your feet and hands and even your spine by lying on the Earth. Your spine has receivers for electrical energy, unlike other areas of your body.

Many of you love crystals and rocks. There is a reason for this. As stated, the Earth naturally absorbs excess electrical energy that your body cannot process. Your desire to have many rocks around you is your unconscious way of bringing the Earth close to you so it can absorb the extra energy and help keep you in balance. Rocks are a tremendous assistance in balancing your electromagnetic field. When you create a water environment with rocks, you are balancing yourself through the use of two very important elements.

Air

The oxygen-nitrogen mix that you breathe is even more essential for conducting the new frequencies throughout your body. Deep-breathing practices such as yoga or breath meditations will also be essential for balancing the body during these times of accelerated frequency. Retrain your diaphragm and lungs to make full use of their capacity. Continue to breathe deeply and you will learn to shift your stress level.

Stress occurs when you hold a lot of unreleased energy in your body. If you train yourself to breathe deeply, you will be taking in universal energy and expelling excess energy that might be filled with emotional and energetic toxins. This will help you stay in balance. If you live in a metropolitan area, take time to walk into a nearby forest or park whenever you can so your body remembers what it is like to breathe clean air.

As you absorb more oxygen and retrain your body to breathe differently, you provide food for your cells and your brain. This

41

assists your body to more easily make physical changes and teaches it to conduct energy in a more efficient manner. You might also want to play with the idea of having air purifiers or ozone makers in your home to test different air states. These are not meant to be used permanently, but as a way to teach your body to absorb different, more rarefied air, which in turn helps you make the necessary bodily adjustments. Pay attention in your day-to-day life to when you are not using your lungs and diaphragm to their fullest capability. Retrain yourself to take full, deep breaths.

Fire

If you are carrying any baggage—emotional or energetic—you can use the element of fire to help transform it. Let's say that you had a spouse who died and you have not yet processed your grief. The baggage of the unresolved emotion is causing much pain. Make a beautiful bonfire in your back yard. Create a ritual "letting go" ceremony. Using the above example, you can use the element of fire to help release old emotions by doing the following exercise: Take something of your deceased husband (or wife) that still reminds you of your pain. (It should be something that is not necessary to keep.) In a sacred and reverent way, place the object(s) in the fire and say a prayer of release as you watch the flames. *(Note: Please respect your local fire regulations and use caution and common sense when doing this exercise.)*

This sounds like a very simple example, but it is extremely powerful because the element of fire has the ability to transmute energy from one form into another. This can help free you from the baggage you are carrying. When you are free from it, your physical body can make its changes more easily.

Clean out your closets and the trunk of your car. Release anything you are not currently using or do not expect to use in the near future. If it is burnable, burn it. If it is recyclable, recycle it. If someone else wants it, give it to him. During this shift in energy and consciousness it is essential for people to let go of some of the baggage they are carrying.

Lightening the physical baggage in your life is a metaphor for clearing your internal baggage. As you make an effort in your physical reality, your inner reality shifts as well. Imagine that you

are going on a round-the-world trip and that you have two suit-
cases. One is filled with everything you need and the other with
things you fear and things you have not needed for a long time
but still have not released. Most likely you will rarely open that
second suitcase, but you still carry it wherever you go. Imagine
how your physical body would respond to that unnecessary
weight! There would be a lot of fatigue because of those bags. If
you dispose of that one bag, your body would then allow itself to
rest and you would be able to manage more easily.

Many people have been feeling more and more fatigued. This is
because you are attempting to bring some of this baggage into a
more accelerated frequency. Instead of walking through the airport, you are being asked to run. With all of this baggage, you
become very fatigued and your physical body cries out in pain.
When you carry emotional baggage—when you clutter your reality with things that do not serve you—the physical body is directly
affected.

Your physical body is merely an extension of your soul. It is a
translation of your emotional state into physical reality. Therefore
if your house is cluttered, your emotions are cluttered. If your
emotions are cluttered, your body will be cluttered also. Many of
you have unsuccessfully been trying to lose weight. Often this is
because you have been attempting to get rid of the wrong things.
Instead, look to your inner and outer surroundings. Look to what
you are holding onto as baggage and seek to free yourself from
it—whether it is an emotional state or physical objects to which
you are attached—because they reflect an inner state. Once you
transmute this state of being, you will either drop the weight or
no longer be disturbed by its presence.

There we have all four elements: water, earth, air and fire. You
can use all of them to facilitate your transformation. The keys to
transformation exist within you and manifest outside of you as
well. They are all around you no matter where you look. These
elements are gifts from the Earth Mother to help facilitate your
transformation into wholeness.

Movement is another tool beneficial to your physical body during this transformation. All of you are channeling a tremendous
amount of energy through you right now. Imagine sitting rigidly
while being continually pumped with new energy. The energy

would build, with no release. At that point you would start to experience an unusual form of energy overload. This overload might manifest as low-grade fevers, misaligned vertebrae, or even emotional distress. Each person reacts to the buildup of energy in a unique way.

In order balance your energy, you can use movement to help channel it. One example is Tai Chi. It is a wonderful exercise in movement, breath, and channeling of energy. Running, walking, swimming, dancing, and other simple exercises also help you channel energy. If you do not channel this energy though your body, you might experience discomfort. Be creative and choose a movement program that allows you to move, play, and express your excitement while strengthening the body at the same time.

Choose a time for your movement program when your mind is at rest and when you can focus on your movements. It is best not to combine your movement program with duties such as housework or walking the dog because the energy will not channel through you in the same way. Take time for yourself and do whatever form of movement you love to do. Create a ritual for yourself on a regular basis. You will notice differences in your body. Your energy level will be more consistent, with fewer peaks and valleys. At first your energy level might seem to get worse, but stick with it, because it will eventually balance itself.

Outside Influences

Humans often wonder if television and computer work should be avoided. There has been a lot of fear-inducing material published that suggests some sort of nefarious mind-control energy coming to you through your electrical devices. However, in reality it comes down to one very important belief system.

Are you or are you not the creator of your reality? Are you or are you not a victim? If you embrace the information that you can be controlled by dark forces through your electrical devices (or by any means), then you have chosen the role of victim and your reality will rearrange itself nicely to validate your belief that you are a victim. Your reality is entirely self-reinforced through the choices you make. So choose your beliefs carefully lest you create the very thing you fear.

As a whole, household electricity is not the healthiest thing for the human body. However, if you are a normal person with a normal television or computer, it is not likely to create enough damage to be noticed, if it does any at all. If you are a computer user, there are several products that screen out detrimental frequencies. Computers with a liquid-crystal display (LCD) screen (like those on portable computers) are more gentle on the eyes and the body's electrical systems. Radiation screens for regular full-size computer monitors are readily available; they are engineered to block some levels of electromagnetic radiation. Computer and television frequencies are not going to damage you; however, they could slow the detoxification and healing process if you spend hours in front of the screen every day.

All of this, of course, is also dependent upon the belief systems and fears of your conscious and unconscious mind. If you believe even unconsciously that nothing outside you can affect your health, then you could live under a power line and sleep with your computer without harm. The above suggestions are guidelines only, and the ultimate voice are your own beliefs.

If you truly believe that you create your reality and that no one can be a victim, then you cannot subscribe to the idea that something outside you can affect you. It must be one or the other—a belief in your inner power, or in that of external forces. If you believe you are ultimately a victim, then anything can get you. Learning self-empowerment is an ongoing process. Be alert for the unconscious and unhealed beliefs that influence your life in a negative way.

There are many teachings available that promote fear, negativity, and hopelessness. When fearful information is given, you are faced with an opportunity to think about and choose what you really want to believe. Never listen to an outside source without checking it with your own intuitive self. To do this you will need to learn to tell the difference between the voice of your fear and the voice of your truth.

Information that is fearful allows you to process your fears, which is ultimately a positive idea. You will never be affected by anything outside of you unless you believe you can be. This concept and its implications have many levels. As years pass and you continue to grow, the depth of this truth and its ramifications will be revealed to you—not through your mind, but through your soul. This is all about acknowledging your sovereignty, beginning to understand that *you* are the only creator of your reality. No television, computer, or government with a "sinister plot" creates darkness. Darkness is created through one's own unrecognized fears.

Where Belief Systems are Stored

Deep belief systems are stored not only in one's consciousness but in one's body. One storage area is the chakra system, the seven energy centers of the body located along the spinal column and up to the top of the head.

Belief systems about survival (including financial survival), your identity, and your role here on Earth are held in the **first chakra** at the base of the spine. This chakra is the primal energy center. It also helps to keep a human grounded to the physical Earth reality.

Belief systems about sexuality, about male/female energy and relationships are held in the **second chakra**, located between the navel and pubic bone. Any imbalance in a person's masculine and feminine energy is housed here. This chakra is a key to physical and emotional healing.

The **solar plexus chakra** corresponds to matters of the ego and the human emotional body. This chakra represents third density, while the heart chakra represents the nature of fourth density. Many physical ailments such as ulcers and heart disease are in the chest and stomach area because you are making this energetic change. You are shifting from a more gut-centered way of living (more primitive and unconscious) into a more heart-centered way of living (more gentle and emotionally balanced). Your ability to become heart-centered evolves from the work you do as you clear the lower chakras. This is why emotional work and facing the inner shadow is so vital to the transformation into fourth density. Your higher aspects need the strong foundation constructed from the work you have done with the lower chakras.

Belief systems about your ability to love and be loved are held in the **heart chakra**, including negative beliefs about love. One of the top "killer diseases" on Earth is heart disease. The number one difficulty most people seem to have is loving the self! Heart disease, lung cancer, breast cancer, palpitations—any disease in the chest—is connected to issues of love. These blocks in the heart chakra can be related to issues such as fear of loving oneself, or being afraid to love another and thus being totally vulnerable to that person.

Beliefs about your ability to express yourself are held in the **throat chakra**. This chakra gives you the strength to speak your truth. When balanced with the heart, you can speak the truth through the language of the heart.

Your abilities to know, sense, and see intuitively are held in the **third eye chakra** located between the brows. This chakra is often underdeveloped because human society does not value this ability at present. Any beliefs you might have about your ability to be intuitive are held in this area.

Beliefs about your connection to God are held in the **crown chakra** at the top of the head. This chakra represents your spiritual connection to the cosmos. It is interesting to note that in some Earth religions it is required to cover this area, while in others it is blasphemous to do so. For thousands of years, ancient human traditions have sensed the importance of this area at the top of the head.

All the chakras play a vital role in a balanced physical body. As you learn more about them, you will be able to consciously influence their function. More information will be explored about the chakras in later chapters.

Detoxification

Many people are already on programs of detoxification, which benefit you immensely. It helps to use detoxification programs like colonic therapy, juicing, fasting or homeopathics with the supervision of a trained professional. Physical detoxification, in combination with emotional detoxification through therapy, rebirthing or other treatments, will create a strong foundation for change and a clearing of interferences so you can hold the new frequencies. Eliminating interference will, in the long run, be a tremendous boost to your body and electrical system. Because toxins interfere with your electrical signals, when the electrical system is amplified, the toxic interference will also increase.

In your world today, there are many substances that produce toxic interference. Cosmetics with their many chemicals are notorious for adding to the body's toxic load. It is best to use cosmetics that do not contain artificial chemicals. When you use cosmetics that contain many chemical ingredients, your body must work much harder to detoxify itself. Deodorants and antiperspirants are used by just about everyone. Most contain substances such as aluminum that are harmful to the body over time and can also block the lymph system. Please remember that there are plenty of natural deodorants that work very well. You might want to try the deodorant stone or other items available from your health food store. In order to change what manufacturers create and distribute, consumers must send a loud message about the kinds of products they will accept by making their opinions known through what they buy.

Many people have been concerned lately about repeated low-grade fevers. One of the first actions is often an attempt to reduce it. However, the body is heating itself for a very specific reason: to kill organisms and detoxify itself. When you try to stop a fever with drugs, the healing process is halted and the "disease" is submerged deeper into the body.

These low-grade fevers are another symptom of the changes. As your frequency is increasing, so is more heat. Thus low-grade fevers are acclimatizing your body to more electrical energy. If you have a low-grade fever, soak in a tub with Epsom salts. That affects the electrical field and, in combination with the water, draws out toxins, stimulates the lymph system, and assists the fever to run its course smoothly. Even without a fever, you can use Epsom salt baths as a tool to help your transition into fourth density.

An unpleasant manifestation like a cold or fever is not always what it seems. The body often attempts to cleanse itself through its own natural systems. At the same time, the body might be attempting to communicate something to you. These minor inconveniences are neutral; you are not doing anything spiritually "wrong" if you happen to manifest a cold or flu. Allow it to do what it needs to do. It will not inconvenience you in the long run if you cooperate with it. You can allow your detoxification to proceed without stopping it with drugs. (Of course, this information should be used in conjunction with a professional health practitioner of your choice.)

Many people have been concerned about strange visual and auditory sensations like hearing tones and seeing strange lights. Both of these indicate movement into a fourth-density reality. Here is a simple analogy: When you take off in an airplane, there is a change in air pressure. The ear ringing is not related to air pressure, of course, but to the idea of cosmic pressure or cosmic energy changes. The natural sensors of your body perceive changes in any type of cosmic energy and might translate it as pressure. Some people might actually feel lightheaded or dizzy. It is all an aspect of the change in cosmic energy and your body's ability to adapt to it.

The lights you see can have different origins. Humans are becoming more receptive to spirit guides and their higher selves. Frequently multidimensional energy will be strong enough to break through into 3D reality, so you might actually see it physically. Your eyes are also beginning to adapt to a new form of vision that is much more multidimensional. You will eventually see a color spectrum different from the one you see now. This enhanced sense of sight will also include new fourth-density wavelengths that will lead to an ability to see life forms in other realities beyond third density.

A New Paradigm

Third-density reality can be likened to a tightly-woven tapestry. If you were to hold it up to the light, it would look solid. Therefore, to maintain your connection to the light requires a lot of faith, trust, and sensing of the light, because you cannot see it. As you move into fourth density, the tapestry of reality will look different, more loosely woven. When you hold it up to the light, you will see fibers of light shining through it. This is what is happening now as the fourth-density frequencies are making themselves known to more of you. You are seeing the light, so to speak, and this new sight might frighten some and comfort others. Eventually, the light will be blinding to those who do not open themselves to it and assimilate its tremendous healing and integrative powers.

49

Many humans are concerned about their seeming loss of memory in these days of the shift. There is most certainly a rewiring of the brain occurring. In third density you relied on linear thought. In fourth density you will rely on spherical (cyclical) thought. As you transition from third to fourth there is a point where you will have to learn a new way to utilize memory. Learning the new way requires you to give up the old way as you move. You are beginning to relinquish linear thought and mentality while you have one foot in third density and the other in fourth. It might seem as if you are losing your marbles, but you are not. You are actually learning a new game to play with the same marbles!

You see reality as based in a linear time flow—past, present, future. This is how your thought processes are still wired in your brain. Everything is based on a past that has created a present that will then create a future. You have called this *cause and effect*.

This cause-and-effect idea represents third-density reality and thought. For a moment let us resume the previous example of the little bird. He flies above a line drawn on the ground. As he rises higher he exclaims, "Oh my goodness, the line is not a straight line at all! I was just looking at a tiny piece of a greater thing. The line is really curved!"

The bird flies even higher. His vantage point from this altitude causes an even greater astonishment. The bird says, "Oh my goodness! That curved line is not even a line at all! It is a circle!" The bird begins to realize that he had seen only a very small segment of the greater whole, and from that small segment he had created his views of reality. Now that he sees the greater whole, he must adapt his view of reality to incorporate this more profound understanding. From this bird's-eye view, it becomes obvious that using the old linear model can be quite limiting. In seeing the new spherical model, there cannot be a past that creates a present that then creates a future. It must all exist simultaneously.

Does this then mean that reality is a continual cycle during which you merely repeat the same experiences over and over? Let us see what happens if the bird flies still higher. As he does, he sees an even more amazing sight. Instead of a circle, he sees that the greater reality is a spiral! Traveling on this spiral means that you never experience the same thing twice. You experience cycles or seasons during which new opportunities are given for learning and growth. This is how change can occur. This spiral reality is actually much more closely related to a *fifth*-density expression. It is known as the *golden mean spiral.*

Let us put the spiral on its side. There is a gateway at its tip that leads to another spiral in the opposite direction! Many of you have heard of parallel universes. A parallel universe exists within the other spiral and complements it. This model expresses the idea of the dualistic nature of reality of which you are all a part. You have called these polarities positive and negative.

Positive does not mean good; *negative* does not mean bad. If you look for a moment at a dry-cell battery, you will see that one end has a positive charge and the other a negative charge. This does not mean that one end of the battery is good, and the other bad. They simply represent two charges that must be present to complete the circuit necessary to power electrical machines. You all have these dualistic charges within you; they are labeled *male* and *female.* As above, so below.

The template that represents the consensus reality is dualistic in nature, or polarized. You will find that the reality structure takes on the flavor of this dualistic template. There is a gateway in the center of the spiral through which you can pass from one reality to the other whenever you make choices. You integrate the energy of both choices, even the choices you reject. As the natural evolution of your consciousness continues, polarity will be reduced and integration will begin. You actually experience *everything* in creation no matter what choices you make. You evolve through the experiences of the whole.

The linear perspective has served you quite well up until now, but it is time to expand. You will need to change your thought processes. You are beginning to remember things in a different way than you used to, which might cause you to question your unusual memory lapses. You are shifting from a linear perspective of reality to a cyclical one. It is like learning to ride a bicycle without first using training wheels. You will eventually master it and it will become part of you.

As your perspective of reality and your human abilities change, your body must learn to adapt to these changes. Your skeletal structure is changing and rewiring itself. This is why during the transition health practitioners such as chiropractors, massage therapists, acupuncturists, and Rolfers are so valuable. Genetically and cellularly you are carrying the memories of your ancestors. You need a boost to create a new identity for your physical body structure that you will pass on to your descendants.

The professionals who are working with physical restructuring are circumventing a process that would ordinarily take a very long time. If you notice changes in your skeletal structure, do not be alarmed. Again, water will help you to detoxify and shift. Some other civilizations (such as those in the Pleiadian star system) have transitioned from third to fourth density and no longer have bone like yours. Instead they have a strong cartilage far more flexible than bone.

For change to take place in the most optimum way, your emotional bodies need to be as clear and detoxified as possible. (We will address this more completely in upcoming chapters.) These emotional toxins are stored in the physical cells. During physical detoxification, emotional outbursts might be accompanied by spasms, because the body is literally restructuring itself as repressed emotions are released. A key to rejuvenation is total and absolute emotional flow, which humans find quite challenging. People assume that total emotional flow would throw society into chaos. That assumption is partly true, because if you all suddenly released emotionally, the wave would nearly destroy your planet. That wave is simply the *repressed* emotion you have been holding. Once you clear it and get to a balanced state, your unimpeded emotional flow empowers and heals rather than causes chaos.

People have often asked about the value of sacred herbs and substances to help in the personal transformation process. This can work for some people; however, you will find that any substance, even a natural one, only prolongs the process of transformation if the person deeply believes that the power is in the substance and not within the self.

When a substance becomes an external focus for an individual, the transformational power is lost on its deepest level. This is why the ancients had meticulous rituals when they utilized sacred herbs. It ensured that the focus remained on the power of the self and the spirit rather than the herb. You *do not need* anything outside yourselves to have a revelatory experience. If you choose to experiment, it is up to you. However, you do not need a substance to experience deeply profound inner journeys.

Heart Activation

The movement to fourth density from third is analogous to the movement from the solar plexus chakra to the heart chakra. Because of this shift, many people on the planet are manifesting all sorts of challenges to their hearts. As your energy is accelerated, the heart will have to be healed because 4D reality is based entirely on the heart.

At this time your brains and heart/lung systems are experiencing the most rewiring. We stress the importance of movement because using your cardiovascular muscles strengthens the heart. It will then be able to channel more energy and not feel blocked. The heart must become strong on both the physical and emotional levels for it to be able to channel the high-frequency 4D vibrations.

As the heart is activated, the upper chakras will be activated as well, most notably the throat chakra. Many people have been experiencing dry coughs and tickles for no apparent reason. This is also a part of the change that is occurring.

The transformation is calling on you to speak your truth—always and at all costs. This does not mean to hurt someone deliberately, but that you must speak with integrity, kindness, and honesty regarding all of your own empowerment and self-responsibility issues.

Speaking your truth is a great responsibility. Use your intuitive abilities, your higher self, and your guides as helpers in this task. The throat chakra represents guidance being brought into your physical life. This does not mean that you have to develop any new abilities. You might sit in the privacy of your own home, simply tuning in and writing down what you receive. Every time you fail to speak your truth or express yourself clearly, you will eventually feel it deeply within. You might even feel it in the throat or the heart. You will feel the importance of speaking and walking your truth so deeply that you will not be able to live any other way.

The human species is experiencing evolution pervasively, on very deep levels. You can see glimmers of this by evaluating the changes in humanity over the last one hundred years. Some of these evolutionary changes have already begun, but will not be complete for about 300 years. It might be difficult to see them while you are embroiled in chaos. These changes are far-reaching and profound, and only in retrospect will you see the coming decades as a nexus point in human history.

Conception and Internal Cycles

As you move further into fourth density, the actual flow of your life will change. At present you have separation between certain parts of your life—childhood, adolescence, adulthood and the elder years. These are all segmented aspects of the human expression. As you move into fourth density, the boundaries will change considerably. Eventually, women will be fertile until death. You are already witnessing women having children into their forties and fifties. It is conceivable that you might see this particular change by the year 2020.

By way of comparison, the Pleiadian female body is a good example because Pleiadians are your closest genetic relative. Pleiadian females do not have regular menstrual cycles as you do, but a cycle that is emotional or spiritual in nature (what the human menstrual cycle also is at its most basic level). During the time of menses there is an internalization. In some of the Native American cultures the women go into seclusion. This originally had nothing to do with shame or a belief of the males. Its deeper meaning is to honor a deep inner cycle of power. When a female honors this monthly cycle of yin-yang power, she is much more in touch with herself and the planet.

Pleiadian females can create a menstrual flow (to some degree) for their own symbolic reasons. Some might do it for purposes of cleansing, but they do it through their will and inner knowingness. It is not something that happens *to* them. For Pleiadian females, conception is not something that happens *to* them either.

Humans are heading toward the eventual full control of conception. This control is not achieved by having "safe sex" or using technological devices to prevent conception. You will simply evolve to a point where you will know when you are ready to conceive. When females are ready, they will know how to release an egg—there will simply be a knowingness. There might be a

54

recognition of the consciousness of the child or of the timing. Conception is extremely sacred to the Pleiadians. Their birthrate is very low because of their much greater life span. When a conception occurs, it always happens within the correct timing. Humans are moving in that direction as well.

Many women will find their menstrual cycles changing. Your sensing of your body and its cycles will change as well. You might find your need for contraception eventually lessening.

Pleiadian males also have a conscious recognition of their ability to conceive. There is no reason for fertile sperm to be used all the time. When a woman senses the timing, she releases an egg; the man will also release fertile sperm when the timing is recognized. They are keyed to synchronicity and timing.

Conception will become a conscious rather than unconscious act. There are already individuals on your world who have mastered the art of conscious conception and birth control. This process has only just begun. If you had a life span of 300 years, you would see this ability develop rapidly as consciousness expands.

On Earth, inner power connected to cycles of fertility exist for both men and women. That time of power for men and women exists for the purpose of remembering your own spirituality and connection to God. Some religions and beliefs have considered women's menstrual time to be unclean and contaminating. Perhaps this is because it is actually the time when women can naturally connect with their own spirituality. In a male-dominated society, female power was greatly feared and constantly subverted.

Men have their own cycles as well. If a man is with a woman in an ongoing relationship, their cycles usually merge. When she menstruates, it is often the cycle for both of them to go inward. She is simply carrying out the physical representation of that expression. If a man is without a female partner, he manifests his own cycle that is more subtle. It can be felt, if the man is observant, through his own life force as it is expressed sexually. There is an ebb and flow within this sexual life force, at times more dynamic, at times more gentle. This is representative of the male cycle. You would find that if every man and woman on your planet honored their cycle times as sacred and acted accordingly, incompatibility within relationships would be drastically reduced.

The Digestive System

The digestive process will change radically as well. As your bodies shift you will need to ingest different substances. Your cravings for certain foods will change, eventually reducing the desire for meat, because the physical body will no longer prefer that form of protein as a fuel. Some of you are already having trouble digesting flesh. This is only the beginning. Your body will crave foods lower on the food chain, such as algae, fruits, vegetables, and grains.

You will crave more substances grown without pesticides, because your body will begin to reject all nonessential man-made substances. As this happens, your reaction will depend upon your level of toxicity. If you eat a lot of preserved, fried, or dead foods, your toxicity level might be high. In that case, the transformation could be more difficult. If you have a purer diet, the change in your digestive process will be easier. The simple reason for this change? You will be composed of higher and higher frequencies of light (your natural state), and dense matter as a source of fuel will not support the ever-increasing frequencies.

This is not to say that you must immediately change your diet. If you make no changes at all, your diet will eventually and automatically change itself, but you can facilitate the change by being one step ahead to ensure that you experience it with ease. The biggest step is the release of toxins due to preservatives, pesticides, and medicines. Many of you already do this homeopathically. Consuming freshly prepared fruit or vegetable juices first thing in the morning will assist the process.

The Brain and Spinal Cord

The spinal cord is a major conductor of electricity; it is like the plug that inserts into the wall outlet, so to speak. Paying attention to your spine is very important. When you channel a higher voltage of electricity, your meridians need to be clear. Chiropractic is one way to keep these energy channels clear. The full importance of chiropractic is not yet fully understood. It works on the physical, emotional, mental, and spiritual levels to facilitate powerful and deep change.

When a vertebra is misaligned, it might pinch the spinal nerves and block the energy flow to vital organs and body systems. Without that vital energy, the body can lapse into disease. Emotions or spiritual lessons can cause misalignments and consequent pain. Traumatic spinal movement such as an accident can precipitate emotional, physical, and/or spiritual challenges.

The body acts as a giant antenna that absorbs cosmic energy. If the antenna is malformed, its reception can become severely limited. As you evolve and the density of your bones changes into higher light frequencies, misalignments will be less frequent. For now, misalignments are a symptom of the increased energy to which you are being exposed.

Any vertebra can serve as a circuit breaker. As your body assimilates energy, it begins at the first (root) chakra at the base of the spine. The energy moves upward as it travels to the brain. If there are blockages in the body or if the body perceives that the brain cannot handle the voltage, it will flip a circuit breaker, which dislocates (subluxates) a vertebra. This puts pressure on the spinal cord and nerves, with the result that the brain receives diminished energy.

This defense mechanism works in your favor so that you do not have a voltage overload. Because you are now aware that you have the power to assist these body changes (such as by using chiropractic), you can be in command and cooperate with your body to begin accepting the higher voltage. Once these voltages can be assimilated, the circuit breakers will no longer be triggered. The energy will travel effortlessly to your brain in full force.

Your brain needs the energy channeled through the spinal column for shifting the neurochemical composition of your brain. This allows you to experience some of the traits common to 4D, such as increased psychic ability and a more flexible view of time and space beyond the linear perspective.

You have heard that humans use a very small percentage of their brain power. It is not that you refuse to use more; it is instead like a house whose electrical systems have not been fully installed. As the frequencies accelerate and you channel the energy through your body, the installation of electrical systems will begin in full force and your brain will start absorbing more and more cosmic energy.

Once the connections between your brain, spinal cord and the universal energy are made, you will find your perceptions of reality changing. You have perceived reality from a linear perspective up to this time for very specific reasons related to your growth. However, it is time now for the natural evolution of the species to take you to a new level of being that will stimulate changes in your perception of reality. This is the beginning of the *metahuman species.*

When your perception of time changes, it will cause a direct change in your life and actions because you will not be creating reality from the limitation of linear time. You will instead be creating your reality from the limitlessness of cyclical time. This will change your whole life! This higher brain function is now awakening within the human species. It will enable you to perceive parallel dimensions, past lives, and multidimensional thought in ways your ancestors could not even imagine.

Recognizing Physical Anchors

Your natural state of being is one of conscious energy. In that natural state you have the capability of experiencing multidimensional reality in its infinite forms all around you. But your perception of reality changes when you allow yourself to come into the physical plane and be born on Earth. You create the illusion of being unable to sense multidimensional reality. Thus there is a part of you that must anchor yourself here in the physical so you are not distracted by the limitlessness of nonphysical existence. The part of you that serves as an anchor to keep you here focused in this reality is called the human ego.

The human ego serves as your anchor. So-called dysfunction, disease, and addiction also act as anchors to keep you connected to physical reality. These "defects" have been considered negative, but in some ways they are very important to the overall goals of your soul.

Each of you chose your life path before you were born. You also chose the challenges you would experience on this life path. And you also chose your anchors. You chose either a behavioral pattern or a physical condition that could keep you locked into the physical plane. Otherwise you would not have enough substance or denseness of energy to keep you here.

Some people have chosen physical discomfort or chronic diseases that would be just uncomfortable enough to be noticed, yet not get in the way of life. As an example, a condition called scoliosis (curvature of the spine) is very uncomfortable; however, in most cases it is not painful enough to stop someone from working. It is a condition that in many instances cannot be totally cured. It serves as an anchor to the physical plane. Some people have chosen digestive disorders or allergies. A number of you might have chosen something a bit more serious. Though some souls choose these challenges for past-life reasons or for the lessons they wish to learn, the condition might exist only for the purpose of being your anchor to 3D. Often people cannot find a spiritual "reason" for a condition. If that is your case, it is in your best interest to simply go on with your life and use your condition as a growth tool in whatever way you are able.

Humans have also battled with the emotional challenges of alcoholism, codependency, or a controlling personality. The challenge in that case is to better yourself in whatever way you possibly can. This leads to the point where you might actually be able to choose your anchor consciously.

Let us say you are an alcoholic. It is possible to shift that addiction into something that can actually enhance your life. Traits that were previously called negative can actually be turned in your favor and keep you centered and focused so you can do the work you came here to do. Alcohol addiction might even serve as a way to become more spiritual, because it allows a person to take conscious steps of self-responsibility when they choose to rise above their addiction. It also affords an opportunity to serve other people who suffer from the same addiction. This is an example of how a destructive addiction can be turned around and used to help heal the lives of virtual strangers.

There is a fine line between a debilitating addiction (one that keeps you distracted) and a condition that keeps you anchored so that you can get on with life and even be of service. There is no reason to judge yourself if you have not released an unwanted condition. The judgment will only keep you in a low self-esteem cycle, whereas the condition you are judging might be serving a higher purpose unknown to you.

At times when you have felt at one with the universe during meditation, you were most likely able to see or feel the bigger picture and therefore not relate to yourself as a singular being. If it were not for your anchor, you would not return to 3D reality after those transcendent states. The anchor is very slight, but it is enough to bring you back unless it is your time to leave the Earth plane. After a meditation, when you are more focused in your body, you feel the anchor more heavily than usual. People could not process what is needed if they were living in an experience of total oneness. Your anchors are very valuable.

It is all a matter of perception. If it were time for any of you to leave, you would be gone! You are here because you have chosen to experience this reality. The ego is a wonderful anchor and uses the tool of addiction (as well as other emotional and physical challenges) to ensure that it learns its desired lessons to acquire the desired wisdom.

What you consider addictions (the things about yourself that you once judged) no longer appear distasteful when you truly learn to love and respect yourself. At that point you can live with an affliction—scoliosis, food allergies, or alcoholism—while loving yourself. It will have very little negative influence in your life. This is the path of learning to love the self and release judgment.

Not only do humans have an anchor to keep them connected to the 3D reality; so does the planetary consciousness. This anchor can change through time. Right now the anchor for the planetary consciousness is toxicity. The state of toxicity (polluted rivers and oceans, rainforest destruction, nuclear waste, etc.) serves as an anchor to physical reality. This does not mean that healing or clearing that toxicity is wrong. What you learn from your anchors is vital. Eventually you will no longer need them, because your evolution will have broadened your perspective. As you take responsibility for your planet and thus yourselves, synchronicity will dictate that toxicity is no longer needed. You and your planet will evolve together to the next level and anchors will no longer be needed. You cannot force change, for true change is a product of conscious evolution.

Body toxicity can be a personal anchor for many people in this reality, as are toxic thoughts. Your physical planet will choose different anchors during different eras in time. The 3D anchors of the planet often mirror that of humans. If humans woke up tomorrow morning devoid of toxic thoughts about the self, your planet's toxicity level would also be radically decreased. It is all a reflection. Whatever you believe to be true about yourself or your reality are the parameters of your experience.

Most people are not able to see the actual mechanism that keeps them anchored because the ego presents a house of mirrors to keep you from discovering more about yourself. It is often very difficult even to perceive your own addictions, much less understand why they are there. A physical condition (like an allergy) is fairly easy to see. But behavioral patterns and addictions involve humans in a confusing cycle. Trying to understand your problems intellectually will not give you the key needed for deep and total healing.

The simplest advice is that if you have a habit or addiction you wish to change, then change it—even if it means swapping one addiction or pattern for a less harmful one. Do not worry that letting go of the old addiction will cause you to be ungrounded and disconnected from 3D reality. Your ego will see to it that you remain grounded. It is best not to become caught in the mental chatter of trying to figure out the root of your addictions and emotional challenges. Seek wholeness through emotional healing rather than intellectual understanding.

In this chapter we have discussed how the new energies will affect your physical body as well as some of the psychospiritual ramifications of life in 3D. In the following chapters we will address more directly the emotional healing processes necessary for this evolutionary leap in consciousness.

61

6

KEYS TO EMOTIONAL TRANSFORMATION

There are a number of steps you can take to assist the changes happening in your emotional body. The most important is the processing of fear.

The qualities of third density will not fit through the doorway when you move to fourth density. Processing fear is therefore the number one issue, because fear takes up the most room in your extra suitcase and cannot be successfully translated into a 4D reality. If you notice a lot of fearful information around you at this time, it is simply an indication of how much more willing you are to work with your fears. Do not be concerned that something might be out to get you. Instead, give yourself the opportunity to grow and change as you confront your fears. The following exercises have helped numerous individuals release fear.

RELEASING FEAR
(Exercise)

Step One: Ask yourself the question, **"What do I fear?"** Make a list of your answers, and answer this question on several levels. List your physical fears (such as a fear of snakes or bugs) and also your emotional fears (such as a fear of being alone or of being loved). List as many of the fears as you can. Do not stop until you feel a completion.

When you list your fears, pay special attention to what you are writing. Examine the list to see if there is a common theme. For instance, it might be that your greatest fear is of losing control. See if a large number of the fears on your list are simply manifestations of that one greatest fear of losing control. See if you can synthesize the list to create a couple of themes that encompass all of most of the fears you have written.

Step Two: Ask yourself, **"How does this fear manifest in my life?"** Do you attack others? Do you withdraw? Evaluate yourself to discover the behavior pattern you display when you are in fear. This might take some time. If you can understand what behavior pattern is triggered when you are afraid, you can make different choices.

Before you go to bed every night, write down your behaviors during the day that were uncomfortable and did not serve you. Which behaviors and/or emotions did not feel clean? Be honest with yourself. Examine what you have written, asking yourself, "Are any of those behaviors based on fear?" If the answer is yes, then ask, "What fears are they based on?"

For example, if you wrote that you ridiculed or judged your brother, you might recognize that you did so because of some fear. This helps you identify your patterns so that eventually you can catch yourself acting out that pattern and stop it then and there. This is how you can rewire yourself.

Let us say that you have done this exercise and are now aware of some of your fears. You are at a family party and your brother approaches you. You feel afraid because he represents a loss of control for you. He starts talking to you, and you put him down. In that moment you have the ability to stop the destructive behavior because you now have the tools to recognize that behavior and its fear-based origin. In that moment you can rewire yourself so that you will no longer continue to act out this behavior. Several techniques that can assist your work of rewiring will be outlined shortly.

Step Three: Personify your fear. Drawing (rather than writing) addresses the archetypal level in your consciousness. Many of you, feeling that your fear is an unseen and intangible monster, are unable to deal with it effectively. Because you cannot see it, your fear appears larger than life. Because of this uncertainty, you keep yourself immobile. Personify your fear. Imagine it as a person; bring it to a physical level to place it on equal footing with you.

Take a pen and paper; be creative. Give yourself permission to play. Draw what you feel this Mr. or Ms. Fear inside you really looks like. Maybe it looks like a monster with big long teeth. Conjure up your interpretation of your fear in the most complete way you can. Now that you can picture it in your mind, put it on paper.

After you have drawn it and you know what Mr. or Ms. Fear looks like, you have a tool for change. Each time you feel it, visualize this entity in your energy field and then speak with it. This way you are not talking to some faceless blob, but something that is like a real person within you. Remember, it is now on your level; it is *not* larger than you. Talk to it, dialogue with it, understand it, send it love, support it. Hear what it has to say. Forming a relationship with fear will be of tremendous assistance to your emotional healing and transformation.

FACING FEAR
(Meditation Exercise)

Place yourself in a relaxed and comfortable state. Through imagery, journey to a secret place that is all your own, like a cave. Walk into the cave to meet a hooded figure who represents Mr. or Ms. Fear. Look directly into its eyes. Acknowledge that it is a part of you. Feel a connection to it. Allow yourself to send it love. Allow yourself to embrace it, draw it within you, and transmute it with your own light. You can get very creative with this if you choose. There are no rules of the game other than those you invent. Listen carefully for any dialogue that might occur between you and fear.

Mr. or Ms. Fear expresses itself on an archetypal level, interacting with your unconscious mind through feelings, thoughts and patterns, not words. This exercise gives it a shape and voice so it can begin its healing on a foundational level.

SHOCK VALUE TECHNIQUE
(Exercise)

Among the different techniques that can help you stop destructive and self-sabotaging behavior is the *shock value technique*. At the moment when you find yourself giving in to fear by behaving destructively (such as using ridicule), stop your reaction and take a deep breath. If you are in an awkward place, find some privacy like a restroom.

When you are alone, engage in a behavior that is extremely unusual for you—something that does not fit in your reality. An example might be to take off your shoes and socks and put your feet one at a time under the cold water faucet in the restroom. Think of other shock-value activities that suit your personality. (Doing cartwheels on your front lawn would also be appropriate!)

♢   ♢   ♢

This exercise will cause your subconscious (which normally runs a repetitive tape loop) to stop and say, "Wait a minute! What's going on?" The moment you have the attention of your subconscious is when you should communicate with it. When your feet are under a faucet and your subconscious is wondering, "What the heck is happening here?" is a perfect opportunity to begin reprogramming yourself. The automatic tape loop played by the subconscious will then be replaced by a constructive behavior you choose that supports you rather than pains you or others.

So there you are in the bathroom with a foot under the cold running water. Begin thinking and feeling the following: "I no longer choose to take out my fear on other people. I take 100 percent responsibility for my fear." Say this over and over again. Mean it! Feel it emotionally at the same time you are doing this strange behavior. Your subconscious will begin repatterning itself to this new program.

You will need to repeat your reprogramming often at first. The more often you interfere with your undesired patterns, the sooner you will notice changes in your behavior. Your subconscious will literally be rewired. Most dysfunctional behavior in society is based on fear, whatever it may be—for each person is quite creative in what they choose to fear.

If fear can be processed and transmuted, the potential of who you can become is truly limitless!

The emotional patterns of the third density can no longer be carried the same way in fourth. (It is like trying to carry the heavy suitcase while running through the airport.) So, whenever you feel tension or friction from the movement to fourth density, it is likely because you are attempting to carry something into fourth density that can exist only in third—some aspect of separation. Fear and judgment are emotional patterns representative of the energy of separation, which is a denial of a part of who you are.

Here is a paradox: *What you fear most is also what you desire most!*

All fears eventually need to be integrated and healed. For instance, let us say you are paranoid, and what you desire most is what you also fear most. It is possible that what you desire most is true freedom and self-responsibility, and that your paranoia is trying to give you the message that you want to be free and self-responsible. However, you keep creating a situation in which you perceive something is out to get you. Being paranoid is not being self-responsible, but giving your power to something outside of yourself. It binds you to the very thing you fear and try to avoid. Ultimately, however, your fear and paranoia can be your teacher.

This fear will stay with you until you move through it and approach the one thing you truly fear, the one thing you truly want to become. If you can examine your fear and paranoia, you will realize that they represent the opposite side of what you truly hope to achieve—becoming fully sovereign. Your fear is *always* a sign-post leading you to what you want to become.

Learn to be confident in expressing fully who you are from your heart. If everyone on Earth expressed their hearts fully, the entire planet would change because people would then be honoring their true selves, forcing each of you to honor the true self of others.

When you are not fully expressing yourself through your heart, in a sense you are living a lie. You present a facade, and that facade is what the other person sees. Then both of your facades simply react to each other; your true selves are not even connected. When you never fully express you are, you begin to create the illusion that you are totally separate from each other. The true self of a human is basically good and loving and would never deliberately harm others. Only the facade (a product of the ego) can be frightened and confused, creating manipulation and disharmony. When a society allows its facades to run the show, societal chaos and eventual breakdown ensues.

Most people use fantasy to visualize the things they desire. They have sexual and romantic fantasies as well as fantasies of success. However, there is a flip side of fantasy—*negative fantasy*, which actually has many positive uses.

Releasing Fear through Negative Fantasy

Negative fantasy is a method by which humans can play out the energy of conflict or fear in a nonthreatening way. Positive fantasy is a method for humans to play out desires, needs, and hopes in a positive way. Both of these concepts are important for balance.

Here is an example of negative fantasy: You are worried that your mate is going to leave you. The scenarios that your fears create are considered *unconscious negative fantasy*. You might find yourself running these negative stage plays in your head and emotional body, and then react to them as if they have already happened in the physical. These fantasies have plagued many people. Some feel that they cannot disengage from the negative spiral of these thoughts.

There is a very simple technique you can do to handle these fears. It will seem illogical and dangerous at first, but this powerful technique—conscious negative fantasy—can release you from a negative emotional spiral.

When you begin an out-of-control spiral of negative thoughts and fears, you give energy to an undesired probability through your constant worry. When these fears come up, you chastise yourself for their existence, and try to repress them. Because they are never confronted, the energy behind them is simply repressed. The only way to release this energy, thereby stopping the cycle of negative fear and worry and returning to a healthy, balanced state of being, is by confronting these so-called demons.

Humans naturally engage in negative fantasy during their nightly dream states when their conscious minds are no longer in control. One might have continual dreams of violence or of one's mate leaving, then fear it might be prophetic, but usually these dreams are the natural process of negative fantasy, which confronts the issue and releases the energy. When you refuse to confront an issue in your waking life, you will notice that its occurrence in your dream state will increase, because the energy *must* be released somehow. Negative fantasy in your dream state is beyond your ego's control. However, you can utilize those principles in your waking state to clear repressed emotion even more directly.

To clear these repressed emotions, enter a meditative state and begin consciously creating in your mind's eye the scenarios that you fear. This forces you to confront the issue and process it. Exaggerate the fearful scenarios. Take yourself to the worst possible scenario and watch as you find creative ways to resolve it. Continue this process until you feel an emotional shift.

Humans worry about negative fantasy, afraid that if they fantasize about a negative experience, they will create it. This is not the way reality creation works. *You create only the circumstance to which you give the most energy.* If you repress a fear, you end up creating what you fear because you expend so much energy in repressing it. If you use negative fantasy as a technique to bleed off repressed energy, you actually clear the energy that would otherwise cause you to create the very thing you fear.

Let us say that you get a call from the mortgage company. The clerk says that you owe a large amount of money, but you know that is absurd. When you hang up the phone and begin doing the research to clear your name, emotion wells up and you build an elaborate scenario in your head about what you will have to do to clear it up. At this point negative fantasy takes control. You begin to worry about your home being repossessed and all other exaggerated situations. You are not allowing yourself to direct your negative fantasy for your own good. Instead, negative fantasy is controlling *you*.

Take time each day to evaluate whatever fears you have experienced, and if something has come up that day, devise a brief negative-fantasy technique to help clear your unresolved fears. If you set aside a special time for this inner work, you will reduce the negative fantasy and worry in your waking life. The time you spend in worry mode will begin to lessen considerably and you will gain an understanding of reality untainted by fear and negative fantasy. This will lead to a more realistic view of your own powerful abilities as a creator.

Remember: *Utilizing negative fantasy will not draw the negative circumstance to you.* It will instead free you from the grasp of your fear. You will stop reacting to life from a negative picture of your own making. You will be able to *respond* to life, which is the true meaning of the word *responsible*.

If there are truly no victims and all beings are sovereign, then every emotion you feel is yours and yours alone. No one has made you feel a certain way. You have *learned* the behavior of blaming and victimization in order to defend yourself against a perceived attack. If you can learn to have relationships where nothing is taken personally and be totally devoted to growth, the foundation of your lives on Earth will literally shift. You will see each other for who you truly are, and you will discover that there is nothing to fear. Being responsible also means owning your own pattern of manipulating and controlling others to protect you from what you fear.

Building Profound Intimacy

The statements above might lead you to think that if everyone were truthful all the time, all relationships would fall apart. That is not what happens when truth is spoken fully from the heart. In the past, "truth" was used as leverage in a relationship to get revenge or to prove oneself right. This type of truth is just a facade. It is possible to rebuild these old, disharmonious relationships, but for a solid foundation they must be built upon true honesty from the heart.

This means that humans must mature to have healthy and responsible relationships. It is up to you. Do you choose to have relationships the rest of your life based only on a facade? It is very safe there, which can be enticing. But is also very limiting. You can choose instead to have relationships built on a solid foundation of truth and trust. With truth comes trust. As trust builds, your relationships will become limitless. This leads to true intimacy.

You cannot expect to live comfortably in fourth density if you have intimacy challenges. Third density is based on separation, secrecy, and fragmentation. You can shut down in third density and maintain your safety zone for a while, but because fourth density is based on reintegration, intimacy must eventually be allowed or your evolution will stagnate.

Society will eventually mature and become capable of profound intimacy, where there can be no secrets. Without secrets there can be no lies. Without lies there must be total vulnerability. For that to happen, society must be willing to see itself in all its beauty and ugliness. Each person must be willing to see himself in the eyes and heart of every other person. Humans *will* mature to this point; it is just a matter of time.

It is important that you know what comes with the package of third density and what comes with the package of fourth density. If you choose anything that includes separation, secrecy, or manipulation in any aspect of life, then you get the package of third density and it is perfectly fine if you choose that. However, you need to know what to expect. You cannot have your cake and eat it, too. You must choose either the third or the fourth as a package deal. You cannot mix the options.

In a relationship between two people, one person might want to grow and the other might be afraid of growth. The one who wants to grow begins telling the truth from the heart, which might upset the other person. If this happens to you, you will need to ask yourself which is more important—your relationship (which might be based on a lie), or your full expression from the heart of your true self. Some people choose the relationship even if it is based on a lie. If you choose to maintain a lie-based relationship, remember that you are making a conscious choice and must then accept the outcome. Are you willing to live with that? Recognize that choosing the more limiting reality will be unfulfilling if you wish to walk a path of personal growth. You have the choice of letting yourself become unconscious in order to avoid making life changes. Choosing this option has a high price tag. It is entirely up to you.

One other aspect of truthful relationships relates to "enabling" —when you withhold a truth from someone, a truth that could eventually cause them tremendous growth, because you want to protect them from pain. The only person you are protecting from pain is yourself! You might think it is easier to keep quiet to avoid the chance of being rejected and feeling pain. But in the long run you sabotage yourself and remove an opportunity for growth from your loved one.

To use a rather humorous example, let us say that a woman has come out of a bathroom and her skirt is hiked up in the back. She walks down the street totally unaware of it. Would you feel comfortable telling her? Some people would, but a majority would not. If you speak up and her attention is drawn to it, she might feel embarrassed. You might not want her to feel embarrassed because *you* will seem to be the source of her embarrassment. So instead you let her walk down the street unknowing. The mind and emotions work in very interesting ways! You convince yourself that you are saving her from embarrassment, but what you are really doing is protecting yourself from your own emotions.

It does not have to be this way. The environment of third density can support dishonesty, but fourth density cannot. Secrecy has no place in fourth density. It does not fit and it cannot be carried there.

As you make your choices about what you want to do and how you want to evolve, recognize the package deal that comes with each of your choices. No choice is better than any other. Simply recognize what you are getting yourself into when you make certain choices, and then own those choices fully.

As you move into fourth density you will become more and more telepathic. As you give yourself permission to be open and vulnerable, you will find that ultimately you have nothing to hide because all people are part of the same whole anyway. You will realize that there is no reason to probe another person psychically. There will be a mutual trust created from shared intimacy.

As you are moving toward these changes, one of the most important things you can do is feel your emotions. Humans are very adept at stuffing them. In fact, you are so adept at it that most of the time you do not even know that you are feeling emotions or that you have stuffed them! Begin training yourself in whatever way you can to feel your emotions in the moment they are triggered.

Humans fear that they would always be in chaos if they felt their emotions. However, when your emotions are overpowering and chaotic, it is because *those are the emotions that have been repressed*. When you carry repressed emotion, you can never feel your true emotions in the moment. The chaotic emotions are the ones behind the dam, waiting to burst forth. If you can learn to first work with the emotions you have repressed, then teach yourself to feel in the moment, your emotional flow will be very different. Your emotional expression will be neither harmful nor painful. It will be naturally fluid. The only reason you feel that emotions cause damage is because most of your emotions do not exist in the present but in the past, leaving you swimming in the well of repressed emotions. To some, it might feel like they are drowning.

Integrating Both Polarities

You are now in the process of integrating your conscious, unconscious and subconscious minds toward becoming one living, breathing, holistic entity connected to all levels of existence. Remember that integration means bringing *all* parts into one whole—both the yin and the yang—to achieve true divinity.

Expressing light and love while denying your negativity, your "dark side," is a one-sided, imbalanced approach. As long as negativity is a part of humanity, it needs to be recognized and integrated rather than be rejected and ignored.

Remember the analogy of the battery and its polarities mentioned earlier. Like a battery, you must have both a positive and a negative charge in order to provide the energy for existence itself. Only when both charges are used equally and integrated into oneself can balance and harmony be achieved. Over time you have come to attribute meanings to the ideas of positive and negative. These meanings have evolved into the definitions of good and evil that describe a human perception of the universe, rather than the universe itself.

Judgment is not a universal concept. There is no good or evil outside what you create and perceive through your own experience. The universal energy guides you throughout your life and provides the backdrop for your lessons. However, it is up to you to choose to learn. When you blame another person or do not claim responsibility for your own life, you shut the door leading to spiritual evolution.

Emotion is energy in motion. Repressed emotion is energy that has not been allowed expression. In utilizing the positive and negative nature of the universe, this means that emotions must be allowed to flow in a safe and nonjudgmental environment for the purposes of self-illumination and growth. When this occurs people retain their power as both spiritual and human beings because they learn to value themselves. Without the ability to express healthy emotion, repressed emotions leach away your power until you must look to others as the source of your power.

Reclaiming Personal Power

Many of you have heard the phrase, "Take your power back." What does this truly mean? Let us examine the following dramatic illustration through the use of analogy to clearly demonstrate this concept.

Mary and Joe are a married couple. There have been a lot of robberies in their neighborhood and Mary feels frightened. She decides to take action. One day she buys a cute little pearl-handled pistol and is excited about learning to use it. She comes home and says to Joe, "Look what I bought today! I am going to learn to use it so I can feel secure." At that moment Mary is in her power because even though she is afraid of the gun (the "power") she is committed to becoming responsible and learning to use it wisely.

Unexpectedly, Joe says, "Are you sure you can handle this thing? Last time you tried, you couldn't hit the side of a barn. I don't think you should have this gun." Joe's issues about the loss or diminishment of his own power result in an attempt to return Mary to a powerless state. He is more concerned about having a partner with whom he can feel powerful than a partner who claims her own power.

Mary begins reverting to her old insecure patterns, being influenced by Joe's lack of enthusiasm. She says, "Maybe I made a mistake. I can't learn to shoot. What if I shoot Joe by mistake?" She begins doubting herself.

Mary begins to think about this situation and sees a way out. She says to Joe, "Why don't you hold this gun for me? We'll put it in the drawer and if there is an intruder, you can use it instead of me." Instead of learning to become responsible for her own power, she hands it to someone else to protect her.

Days go by and each day Mary opens the drawer and looks at the gun. She convinces herself that because she knows where her "power" is, she is safe even if she is not the one responsible for it. One day she opens the drawer and the gun is gone. She begins to worry, "The gun isn't here! Joe must have hidden it! If I ever need it I won't be able to find it! Maybe Joe is planning to kill me in my sleep!"

The moral here is that when you give your power away and no longer take responsibility for it, the power to create your life is out of your control. Since Mary was manipulated by Joe to no longer trust her own power, she gave it away (thus making Joe feel powerful). Suddenly Mary no longer knows or remembers where her power lies. She has lost sight of it and has probably become too afraid to confront Joe. Asking him to return the power is humiliating and frightening, so Mary will spend her nights and days worrying about the location of her power, never realizing that the ache in her heart is not because the gun is missing. The ache comes from her own sense of powerlessness.

This story was specifically chosen because many people in your society have issues surrounding power and especially about guns. Though the gun in the story is meant to illustrate a personality dynamic, please know that guns remain a strong symbol in your society. They are amazing teachers because of the fear that surrounds them. As with any fear symbol, abolishing the thing you fear will never make it go away; it only represses your fear further. Only through confronting your fear will it be transformed. In the case of guns, once the fear is truly confronted and trans- formed (and the issues surrounding it as well) it is likely that your society will evolve beyond its fascination with them.

To generalize, girls are often taught to give their guns (their power) to their daddies, so to speak. When they get older they transfer their power to their brothers and husbands. Men are socialized to believe that the only safe place for a gun is in their possession. These unconscious beliefs are perpetuated generation after generation. The feminist movement is not about women attempting to surpass the power of men, but about reclaiming the "guns" they have surrendered to a male-dominated system for generations. Women simply want to be equal holders of power. From the point of view of some males, this might mean relinquish- ing the guns (power) they have mistakenly believed were origi- nally theirs. This has caused a lot of fear and resistance.

RECLAIMING PERSONAL POWER
(Exercise)

Imagine all the people with whom you have interacted during your life. Write down the names of those to whom you have given your power. Who are the people to whom you have entrusted your security? It could be former lovers, parents, teachers, governments, or churches. After you identify them, ask yourself why you gave it away in the first place. Write down as much as you can and be as honest with yourself as you are able.

♢   ♢   ♢

Many of you have given your "guns" to your structures of government, church, school and so on. These structures protect you from your own fears and feelings of inadequacy. By giving away your power in this fashion, you never learn self-responsibility. As you do the above exercise, you might have feelings of self-doubt. If so, that is wonderful! It is a first step. To achieve self-confidence, sovereignty, and emotional power, you must reexperience the self-doubt from which you gave your power away. Only at that point can you make a different, empowered choice. To get there, you must hold the gun—the symbol of your fear. Thus, you must confront yourself.

Once you know who has your power and where it is located (metaphorically), you are now ready to take whatever actions are necessary to reclaim it. It might mean changing or ending an unhealthy relationship or starting your own business instead of working for an unscrupulous boss. Whatever that point of power means for you is not important. Taking action to become empowered once again is the primary goal.

The phrase "Take your power back" means that you must confront your fears and master them. Once mastered, you once again hold your power and destiny.

Let us return for a moment to Mary and Joe. Once Mary understands her pattern of surrendering her power, she can begin to reclaim it. One day she confidently says to Joe, "Remember that gun I gave you years ago? Do you still have it?"

Joe replies, "Yeah, sure I have it. I've been keeping it for you all these years, waiting for you to want to learn how to use it." Now Mary begins to remember to whom she gave her power and why.

Mary asks, "Where is the gun?"

Joe answers, "It is in the top drawer under my socks." Now Mary knows exactly where she can find it.

At this point it is Mary's responsibility to take the gun out of the drawer when she is ready and decide what she is going to do with it. She might choose to get rid of it. That is a valid option; however, we would suggest that Mary be very clear about her motivation for doing so. (If getting rid of it is based on fear, the cycle will simply be repeated.) In this analogy, Mary chooses a more empowering road.

Mary now begins to see the gun as a symbol of her own power. She willingly takes shooting lessons. She becomes so proficient a marksman and so confident in her ability to master a new challenge that she no longer needs to have the gun. In a sense, she loses interest because of her mastery; it has become a part of her. What she once feared has now been confronted, and because she now feels safe with her newly gained power, she no longer feels a need for a gun. She is afraid no longer. If she chooses to give away the gun, it will be from confidence rather than fear.

This analogy was a long journey to express a very simple truth. You are now in the middle of one of the most important lessons of all. In your spiritual explorations as you move into 4D, you are now doing the following:

- Discovering to whom you have given your power

- Discovering why you gave it away

- Reclaiming it

- Learning to use it without fear.

One reason why many personal empowerment classes do not seem to work for some people is that even though you are learning to use your power, you still have not discovered where you have put it, how to reclaim it, and what that truly means. Often it means tremendous life changes. Before you engage in more empowerment classes, retrace your steps. Find where you have put your power. Bring yourself back to the point of self-doubt and fear. Learn to use this powerful tool even though you fear it. If you do this you will achieve the mastery you are seeking. Fear and insecurity will transform to self-confidence.

If you are able to conquer the fear of your own power, you will no longer be a slave to emotions. Your ego will no longer have to create elaborate scenarios to protect you from your fear and then use a tremendous amount of energy to keep the protection intact. The large amount of energy needed to keep your fears at bay can now be channeled in the direction of your own empowerment. When you make a shift in your internal reality such as the one described, your cellular body begins to change, making it possible to hold the new frequency that you have begun incorporating.

It is up to you to confront the things you fear, whether they are external or internal. The key is to become responsible for your life and for who you are. It is not selfish to make personal growth your number one priority. The world is not going to change unless *you* do! When you talk to your friends, stress the importance of their growth and the attainment of their joy and inner light—not through the rejection of darkness but through the confrontation and integration of it deeply within.

Be there for your loved ones. Be willing to cry together, laugh together and heal together. Reach out as you would like others to reach out to you. If your first priority becomes healing the self, then the nature of that priority dictates that you are also healing the planet. You cannot separate yourself from the Earth. You are one and the same.

7

HEALING THROUGH INTEGRATION

Healing physically, emotionally and spiritually are not separate processes. They are all tied together. The healing issue needs to be addressed holographically from a point of view of wholeness. Because you are a holistic being, every aspect of you affects the whole being.

The relationship between your mental and emotional bodies can be illustrated with a story that demonstrates a very important dynamic in the human psyche. Let us call this first character Susan.

Mental and Emotional Healing

Susan has a fear about driving and riding in cars. Whenever she is in a car, she feels terrified. Susan asks for assistance from a hypnotherapist and explores her past lives. After finding out that she was killed in a carriage accident in the 1800s, she begins to develop an intellectual understanding about this death and why she fears cars.

After some time has passed the fear does not disappear, because she has not shifted her understanding of the fear from her intellect to her emotional body. She thinks she has discovered the answer, but cannot figure out why she is not healing.

More time passes. Susan begins to develop an ulcer. The pain is triggered whenever she thinks about riding in a car. Because her understanding has not yet filtered into her emotional body where it can be healed, a fragment of her personality acts to defend her from the fear. Eventually the body must release the actual energy of fear. It can do this in a variety of ways. One way is through the physical body (by way of any number of ailments) as Susan did.

Physical symptoms are always a direct message that something is not being processed. Symptoms can bleed off energy that you have not processed emotionally. If Susan can bring her intellectual understanding into an emotional understanding, acceptance, and commitment to healing, then she can shift her physical symptoms. When that shift occurs, her healing begins.

Emotional understanding is an inner knowing that is not dominated by the ego or the intellect. If you try to understand this with your mind you will not comprehend it completely. An emotional recognition is *felt* rather than understood. It can be described as an *aha!* sensation, usually accompanied by chills, goosebumps, tears, and possibly a feeling of humility. Once you make the cognition you must relinquish your defenses and stay open and vulnerable emotionally and mentally for healing to occur. Letting go of your defenses might trigger more emotional pain, but it is a powerful, necessary, and ongoing part of your healing.

This emotional recognition is essential to the process of physical healing, for the intellect cannot do it alone. Integrating the mental body's understanding with the emotional body's recognition will shift the pattern so that Susan can then manifest her healing through whatever modality she chooses.

The emotional body does not process data linearly. In third-density reality, that is the job of the mental body. The emotional body's processes are holographic. That is why it can be affected by things that have happened to other aspects of your soul in other lives and dimensional realities. It is also why you can still be affected by earlier traumas in your life.

Susan recognizes that her fear of cars originated with her carriage accident in the 1800s, but this knowledge cannot shift her fear. She needs to experience the depth of emotion surrounding that carriage accident so that it can be cleared. It is unnecessary for Susan to believe in past lives to make this shift. In the unconscious (where the psyche responds to archetypes and metaphor) all that is needed is the story alone because it carries such a strong charge for her. Whether it is "real" or just a story matters little, because her psyche responds either way.

Susan returns to the hypnotherapist, regresses to the life in the 1800s, and gets in touch with those emotions. If she totally commits to her healing and completes this process, she will eventually reach an emotional cognition that will allow her to understand holographically why she is afraid of cars. This understanding will deeply affect her emotional body, stimulating the healing process.

This experience will align her with who she was when she experienced the carriage accident. It means she will temporarily become a past Susan. When this happens, a cognition will occur on deep levels that will require her to understand why she chose to experience the accident. She will own her reality in a multidimensional, holographic way that is essential to total healing. This shift will filter through all her other incarnations and compartmentalized aspects until it becomes fully transformed. At this point mental, emotional, spiritual and physical integration begins.

Many people who embrace a new-age philosophy continue to have pain because they mask it with love, light and sweetness. This tactic never truly heals the pain. These people have embraced an unbalanced "love and light" doctrine that "feels" good intellectually and seems to make sense. It is comforting to believe (erroneously, of course) that they do not have to feel the pain in order to heal, so they surrender to a process that builds a facade—behind which the wounded heart remains.

What about the emotional body and its needs? What about the abused child inside? What about the unresolved pain that longs to emerge from the shadows to be recognized, owned, loved and released? Pain cannot be healed by the intellectual acceptance of a chosen doctrine. Religions cannot be an instrument for true healing if they are embraced only on a surface level. *Dogmas and doctrines have promoted intellectual acceptance at the expense of emotional and spiritual revelation.*

If Susan begins to see the gap between her light and love philosophy and her inner pain, she will approach a powerful and liberating transformation. When she wallows in the mud emotionally and releases the raw energy that has been repressed for so

81

long, she will begin to understand the true concept of universal love—which includes embracing the total human experience, including the darkness.

There is nothing inherently wrong with a light and love philosophy. It has simply been misunderstood that this meant denying the darkness and pain. When the whole of the human experience is embraced—the light *and* the darkness—the result is a tremendous amount of true, clear love coming from a healed heart rather than a wounded one.

Many new-age belief systems are replete with lingo that satisfies only the mental body. Individuals are adept at intellectually understanding concepts such as "You create your reality" or "What you put out you get back," but these words do not lead to emotional and spiritual understanding. Those words present an intellectual framework but do nothing for the pain. Many people have deep fears about accepting total responsibility for their reality. They understand the concept mentally, but emotionally it terrifies them.

All of you are living, breathing sparks of creation. You have the right to grow and integrate all aspects of yourself. This is why you have entered into this journey of spirit. If you are experiencing emotional pain, it is a sure bet that you are resisting a truth about yourself or your reality, using the intellect as a screen to keep you from seeing or feeling your emotions.

Some people never feel pain because their emotions are so well guarded. The ego is an expert at self-deception, declaring truthfully, "I feel no pain; I'm fine." Be careful about declaring you have nothing to heal, because it is a sure sign that an emotional revelation is hiding under the surface.

The mental body is currently like a driver that holds the reins of the inner processes of the human psyche in third density. It is attempting to navigate you and warns you about what is on the path ahead. Meanwhile, the emotional body sits warm and comfortable inside the carriage, believing the driver knows what he is doing. In a state of dependency, it never looks out the window to see for itself, but allows the mental body to protect it and make the decisions. When the emotional body (the part of you that can allow itself to be vulnerable and thus ready to heal) finally looks out the window and learns to see clearly, the healing process will begin.

Achieving Sovereignty on Earth

Achieving sovereignty means taking total emotional responsibility for your healing and transformation on all levels. Because you are an expanding being, you can always love yourself a little more. There is never an end to how much you can grow or how much you can love yourself. Love and growth are expressions of expansion. You are moving toward true peace, healing, and sovereignty, byproducts of undistorted self-knowledge.

Only when humans respect themselves and their sovereignty can they respect the sovereignty of others. Until then there will always be conflict. It starts within the self. If everyone lived by the ideals of self-respect and self-love, the entire planet would be transformed overnight.

You are not experiencing the conflict of polarities as a planetary species because you were "bad" or disobedient and "fell from heaven." You are part of a grander scheme, one of healing on a galactic family level. If your father is an alcoholic, it is likely that someone in his family was one also. You are now beginning to see how dysfunctional patterns are passed down through the generations. Your extraterrestrial genetic forefathers were young when they gave birth to your species, and they passed on some of their unhealed patterns to you. You then created further unhealthy patterns of your own.

Ultimately, all of this is for the growth, expansion and healing of the entire family dynamic. What you are accomplishing on Earth at this time is truly a miraculous transformation. Your forefathers have tried to heal this before in many different planetary systems, but they were never able to heal these patterns of dysfunction. You are an extension of them, and you therefore bring forward many lessons they did not complete. When you embrace these lessons and take responsibility for your own healing as individuals and as a planet, you will have achieved the sovereignty that your forefathers lacked.

The nature of physical reality on Earth is like a house of mirrors. It is as if the fragmentation necessitated by this reality was so

83

jarring that you needed defenses to soften the blow of leaving your natural nonphysical state. When you first entered this system on Earth, it was as if you walked into an empty room. In the room there was one mirror, and you saw yourself clearly in it. But what you saw was very painful because it was tainted with the whole of humanoid experience.

You saw self-judgment, self-hate, shame and guilt, and the pain was too much. You shattered the mirror. Now all the pieces of the shattered mirror reflect light from many different angles. Thus every time you look in a mirror you can't tell whether it is a direct reflection or a reflection bounced along the hall of mirrors.

You are in a reality where it is difficult to differentiate between your true reflection and one that has been distorted by your ego's protective mechanisms. These mechanisms can lure you away from who you really are. The challenge is to recognize your true reflections, and this requires endless and honest self-examination. Many of your reflections hold pain and shame whereas others hold a profound beauty. You have had difficulty accepting both the pain *and* the beauty you carry. Your challenge in this house of mirrors is to see yourself for who you really are. As you begin, your facades fall away and you will learn the deeper meaning of self-love.

LOVING THE REFLECTIONS
(Meditation Exercise)

Put yourself in a quiet meditative state. Imagine walking down a long corridor and standing in front of a door. Open it and walk inside. Within that room is a beautifully ornate mirror. Walk over to it and look at your reflection, the one you see every day, a full-length image. Search every detail of that reflection as if you are scrutinizing it for the first time. Do not be afraid to look in the most private of places.

Now change the reflection. Instead of seeing your usual self, consciously change this reflection into the "ugly" you. If you are afraid of being fat, make the reflection obese. If you do not like your nose, make it even more ugly than you think it is. Create a grotesque caricature of your day-to-day self. Know that you are in control of what you see. Stare into your eyes without fear or revulsion and note how this makes you feel. Know this image inside and out. Own your feelings about it; do not tuck them away. This is a part of you created by your own denial, fear, and negative thoughts. Accept this person who lives inside you, because *you created* that being.

Look into the eyes. Notice the tears, because that being is now vulnerable, feeling exposed and naked. The reflection desperately wants to be loved and is reaching out to you for acceptance and unconditional love. In its eyes see a spark of light, that total integrated you, your God-self, lying behind the pain. Recognize your true self in that spark. Extend love to it. Put your hands up to the mirror and touch your reflection. Love it more than you have ever loved any part of yourself.

As you pour love into this reflection, watch as it begins to change. It is absorbing your love like a sponge. It begins to change into the you that you have wanted to become. Continue this process. Now step back from the mirror and watch how your reflection alters itself to a more enlivened and fulfilled one, yet one that does not cause you to feel threatened by its newness. This reflection is slightly more joyous, loving, confident, and integrated than your previous self. The light shining from its eyes is very warm and open. Merge the light from its eyes with the light coming from your own. In that moment you join paths. It becomes you. Relax in this sacred space until you feel the process is complete.

✧ ✧ ✧

Enabling a Problem to Continue

Let us examine a fictional character called Harry who chooses to come into this life with the goal of learning about personal power. His soul has made this choice for its own growth. Harry incarnates on Earth and later in life manifests alcoholism. He surrenders his power to alcohol so that, on a soul level, he can play out the role that will teach him about his power. However, on the conscious level he is unaware of the bigger picture, so his alcoholism is seen as a problem or challenge.

To some degree people will deny the thing that could heal them the most, which includes seeing a direct reflection of who they are.

85

The exercise above allows you to see reflections of yourself that are true and others that are distorted. It allows you to see that you *can* survive the experience of the pain or ugliness within you, and that it does not have to be feared.

Harry's wife and children never want to hurt his feelings. They never tell Harry that his behavior is inappropriate. They never tell him that his actions cause them pain or that they think he is in denial and offer their help. Instead, they act as if everything is just fine and that alcoholism is part of normal life.

Let's say Harry goes out and wrecks his car one night while driving drunk. Harry's mother says, "Oh no! Harry doesn't have a car now. He can't go to work and support his family. I'll give him the money to fix his car so he can keep his job and support his family."

Though this might seem like an act of love, Harry's mother actually helps him to avoid the consequences of his actions. She is really attempting to take responsibility for her son's reality, whereas the only person who can really take responsibility for Harry's reality is Harry himself. By fixing his car, Harry's mother is allowing him to repeat the cycle of irresponsibility. She will most likely lend him the money over and over again after each mishap. The cycle continues because no one will ever allow Harry to face the consequences of his actions.

This type of interaction is known as *enabling*. Harry's family enables him to continue his pattern so he can never fully experience the consequences of his own actions. If it is true that his goal for this incarnation was to learn about empowerment, how can he do so when no one ever gives him the opportunity to take responsibility for himself and his actions? A true act of love on the part of Harry's family would include anything that would allow him to see a clear reflection of himself. Once Harry can see himself clearly, he can consciously choose to take responsibility for his life. This results in tremendous growth. If Harry's family refuses to do this because they do not want to hurt his feelings, could it be that they simply wish to avoid conflict and conveniently justify their failure to take action?

The pattern of enabling in the human race is very deep. It exists in everyone to some degree. This is a dramatic example, but it occurs frequently and in even more subtle ways. How many times have you been with someone you love very much, and they continue to dwell on a life drama that is not the true source of their pain? You sit and listen, nodding your head, but you never say to them: "I love and respect you, but I feel the source of your pain is (fill in the blank). Your pain isn't because so-and-so stabbed you in the back; it is because *you* don't like the reality you created through your choices and actions. Take a good look at yourself."

Harry never gets the opportunity to see his own pain or ugliness (which is a vital part of him) because everyone is too busy protecting him from it. He must see that denied reflection of himself in order to heal. Enabling is one of the reasons why family dysfunction is perpetuated. Why would someone continue to enable? Perhaps seeing the powerlessness in someone else reminds them of their own feelings of powerlessness. Thus the cycle is never broken.

Be aware each day when you might be enabling. Pay attention to when you withhold something because you do not want to hurt someone who just might benefit from your honest feedback from the heart. If you stop withholding and you say what needs to be said out of your love and caring for another person, then you stimulate their growth in a tremendously empowering way. You become an active cocreator in his growth because you do not withhold the reflection that he needs to see in order to make changes. Of course, this requires the height of diplomacy, love, and integrity. If your words cannot be said from the heart, it is best that you wait until you can say them with love. If you are not ready to speak purely from love, there are ways to stop enabling even while remaining silent.

Enabling patterns exist in family and interpersonal structures, and also exist on a societal level. Let's say there is a country being destroyed through famine and the people cannot help themselves. You have several choices. One choice is to ship supplies to them, but that is only a temporary solution. Once the supplies are gone, they are hungry again. This can be a form of enabling because they never get to see that they can solve their hunger by becoming empowered. So instead of providing a temporary solution, you could send them teams who could teach them how to feed themselves. The ancient proverb describes it well: *If you give a man a fish, he can eat for a day. If you teach him to fish, he can eat for a lifetime.*

Many people give each other assistance through enabling, a temporary bandage. This is a continual drain of the giver's energy, and the individuals who accept that assistance never achieve their own empowerment. Instead, they become dependent on the assistance. Other than in emergencies, is this truly the best form of assistance?

If you look at the challenges in nearly every country of the world, you will see at least one situation of enabling. Most individuals enable to avoid feeling powerless to change things. This has led to "fixing" the situation by the most readily available method, albeit temporarily.

The expedient solution does not address the idea that everyone needs to think of themselves as individuals *and* as a community. Few people have wanted to take total responsibility for their reality because they have become so enmeshed with each other that they have been unable to see a clear road to their own sovereignty. You as humans really do have the ability and strength to help yourselves and others in a way that will truly be of service.

Your neighbor is a reflection of you. If he is hungry, it is an ugliness you do not want to see in yourself. Hence, you feel the need to cover it up quickly before it can be acknowledged. When you recognize that your neighbor is a direct reflection of you and accept the pain you see as present within you as well, you can truly, cleanly, and with integrity assist your neighbor. However, you cannot truly assist another being if your underlying motivation is to make *yourself* feel better.

ENDING THE ENABLING CYCLE
(Exercise)

Keeping a journal will help you identify instances of enabling in your life. At night when you go to bed, log every instance in which you might have enabled someone else during that day. Record every instance during which you withheld your true self and opinions from another person. Log it and own it. Also log every instance in which you have acted with integrity, where you have been honest, where you have stated your truth with love. You can help another see a reflection of themselves when you act with honesty and love. You give them a true gift.

⚬　　　⚬　　　⚬

There is a great responsibility that comes with this knowledge. Each of you has a responsibility to make sure that your motivations are pure before you speak to another. You must clearly know that your words come from love rather than a desire to change the other person. Your words must not be prompted by a desire for revenge or to belittle him or her to boost yourself. You must have no attachment to his reception or rejection of the information. You must remain in your own sovereignty and not try to force him to see the reflection you present. Ask yourself "Am I more interested in getting him to admit I am right than in his healing?" Finally, you must be prepared to be wrong about your observations. Wrong or right, your words set into motion a chain reaction toward healing if both parties engage in dialog willingly and with enthusiasm. If you can master all of the above and be humble, you will have learned one of the most difficult-to-master tools gained from the human experience.

As you gain experience in using this tool, your defensiveness will drop. You will be able to hear and speak without insecurity. The fine art of using this tool requires the relinquishment of ego and a focus on the heart. The irony, however, is that when most people think they are acting without ego, they are not. If you are truly acting without ego, you will have no emotions other than compassion and love, and you will have no attachment to the outcome.

True Partnerships

A true partnership is one in which each partner can listen without defensiveness and speak without fear of retribution. This requires mutual trust. It requires that you take off your armor, trusting you will not be attacked. It also requires that you stop attacking the other person no matter what the circumstances. You must be honest about your true motivations. As the mass consciousness on the planet changes and expands, this will become easier.

If you must deal with someone who cannot hear your words, the language they *will* understand is the language of action. Actions speak to the unconscious. For instance, instead of saying to the person, "You drink too much alcohol," allow your actions to demonstrate that you will not tolerate that behavior from them any longer. You might also emulate the behavior you wish to instill in your loved one, as long as you do not lose your own sovereignty in doing so. Acting with integrity is the only way you can come to peace within yourself, even if your loved one chooses not to change. *You must be true to yourself, or you can never be true to anyone else.*

When one claims personal sovereignty, reality *must* change. If Harry's wife tries to claim her sovereignty out of anger or revenge, it will not work. She must do it from a recognition of the need to create it for *herself* rather than change him. It always comes back to *you*.

When Harry's wife takes her sovereignty, several things might happen. There will be a noticeable shift in her emotional patterns. If it is a ruse of the ego wherein sovereignty has not been claimed on the inner levels, everything will stay the same. If sovereignty is truly claimed, then either (1) Harry will shift, (2) she will shift enough to remove herself from the situation, or (3) the alcoholism will not bother her anymore.

Each individual (including the enabler) is in a given scenario for their own healing, not necessarily for the healing of others. You cannot ever heal another person, only yourself. This is why healing on a personal level is so critical. As you heal yourselves, you heal the planet. You cannot heal the planet if you refuse to look at yourself, because your planet is a reflection of who you are.

8

CHANGE YOURSELF,
CHANGE YOUR REALITY

Before you ventured into the world of physical experience, you existed in your natural, original state as a nonphysical field of consciousness. In that reality you did not have to worry about how to create your reality because whatever you thought immediately *became* your reality. In your natural nonphysical state, there is no time lag as there is on Earth. Creations are instantaneous.

The same mechanism that creates reality in the nonphysical state also creates reality in your physical state, but the illusion of time and space causes a time lag in the physical. There appears to be a long waiting period between thought and reality. You have chosen that "delayed action" in physicality to teach you many valuable lessons.

Creating Your Reality

Creating your reality is truly a one-step process. This step can be defined simply as **be that idea**. *Be* the idea you want to create, in whatever way is available to you.

This one step by itself is all you really need to create any new reality. For the purpose of analysis and illustration, however, this one step will be broken down into six minor steps so that you can examine each facet of the process.

Take a moment to choose something that you wish to create in your life. However, do not choose a *thing* (like a car, a house or a mate). Things are really extensions of inner states of being when they appear in your life. Instead, choose a *state of being*. This state of being will, when manifested in physicality, bring to you the *thing* that your ego desires. For instance, the state of being called mobility might bring you a car as well as positive personal traits. If you choose to focus on being more loving, that might also bring a mate to you, among other positive experiences. One cannot ever truly create things without first creating the state of being in which they can exist.

The emotion behind the desire to create a given situation will always dictate the actual outcome. This can backfire if you are not aware of the root emotion involved when you create your manifestation. For instance, if you desire a relationship because deep down you are afraid of being alone, then you will continually create a state of loneliness. The emotion behind the attempt at manifestation (in this case the fear of being alone) actually puts *more* energy into the reality of being alone. Emotions always speak louder than words.

Also, you can never be dependent upon another person to create a desired reality. For example, you cannot create with integrity a situation in which a specific person and no one else must be your mate. Your desire in such a case would not be pure. Creating a reality (a *state of being* rather than a *thing*) is your responsibility alone. If your desire can be fulfilled only by the actions of another person, you are attempting to fulfill an ego desire. Ego desires cannot be fulfilled by using universal principles. The ego does not understand—and even fears—the nonphysical world of the soul. Thus it will continually sabotage the very thing it thinks it wants!

CLARIFYING YOUR DESIRES
(Written Exercise)

Write down the state of being you wish to create within yourself. In addition, write down what *things* or *life conditions* this state of being might create for you in physical reality. The act of writing helps to ground your thoughts into physicality and has the power to help magnetize your desires to you. Here is an example of the completed written exercise:

I wish to create the ability within myself to become more loving. If I were to become more loving, the following might manifest in my life:

- *a life partner*
- *a healthy sense of self-worth*
- *a career in which I am valued*
- *friends who love me*

Begin to think and feel what having these uplifting conditions would be like in your life.

✿　　　✿　　　✿

Step 1: Act As If

The first step is to *act as if*. In other words, let's pretend for real! In terms of how the universe views your actions, there is very little difference between pretending your reality and truly creating it. Pretending is a way to begin to know how your preferred reality *feels*. As you begin to understand how it feels, you are more than halfway there.

After you know how the desired reality feels, *begin acting as if it is real* even more frequently and earnestly. At what stage does the pretending stop and the "true" reality begin? This cannot be measured. Trying to do so will only give you a headache! It truly does not matter. Pretending your desired reality is really just a process of building your own personal training wheels to teach you how to be a conscious creator.

Let us say that you want to create success in your life. You must do all of your homework to find out exactly what success means to you. Once you have done that, begin pretending you are a success in everything you do. This requires dedication and the willingness to let your childlike, playful self emerge.

You will need to silence proclamations by the negative ego that seem to convince you that you are failing. Perhaps you have a pattern of continually (consciously or unconsciously) reinforcing your failure to do anything right. Perhaps you enjoy a personality drama where you go into a slump, walking around pouting about what a failure you are and how for once you would really like to be a success. However, be careful of indulging in negative thoughts, because you will in fact manifest the idea of success

93

through a negative framework—by continually "succeeding" at failure!

Let us say that your ultimate goal (in terms of physical manifestation) is to take a job as a book editor. However, right now you are living in a town where there is no publishing industry. Instead, you are working in a restaurant flopping pancakes. Here you have a choice. You can flop pancakes with a long face, whine about your fate and complain that you will never become an editor, or you can put all of your energy into flopping pancakes and be the most successful pancake flopper that you know how to be! In that case, you will be *living* the idea of success.

As a successful pancake flopper, you will be acting as if you are a success and therefore every other aspect of your life will follow suit. Because you carry the ideas and energy of success within your life, you will ultimately be a success in everything you touch. *It is that simple!* Achieving an attitude of success means that you know that flopping pancakes is not your fate, but that right now it is merely a way for you to work on certain aspects of yourself until you move into the next phase of your success. Perception and attitude are vital keys in the creation of a desired reality.

You will find that shortly after you begin pretending, you will not be pretending any longer because you will have triggered the true energy of the attribute you are seeking. At this point, pretending is transformed into becoming.

EMPOWERING THE VISION
(Meditation Exercise)

Briefly close your eyes and relax. Think about what you have written down as your goal. In your life right now picture yourself emotionally and energetically acting as if whatever you have chosen is already in your life. For example, if you are a car salesman, watch yourself become full of the energy of success. Feel it as an energy that expands you. Feel the emotion of your goal and apply it to your life today.

When you feel you have come to a peak with that emotion, place your right hand on the area in your body where you intuitively feel your fear is stored. After you have done that, place your left hand on the area in your body where you intuitively feel your

94

strength and empowerment are stored. Now empower the vision you have created. Feel all the fears of your life today being healed and replaced by empowerment and strength.

Watch your vision and goal become more vibrant. Do this as often as you can. As you practice it, you might find that your vision and goal begin to change naturally.

✿   ✿   ✿

It is very important to stay out of your own way. This means that you must allow the natural process to unfold without judging that it is not progressing the way you think it should. Do not make conditional requests of the universe, because the universe is an unconditional realm.

Step 2: Be Unconditional

Many people limit themselves to a demanding "I want it my way or not at all!" This is an ego statement and is not representative of your full, integrated self. The universe is an unconditional place. If you try to place conditions on it, it will create *conditional realities* for you that become extremely difficult to transform.

This is one of the main reasons why humans perceive that they have such difficulty creating. If you ask the universe for something but you say, "It must be *this* way," the universe gets confused, in a sense. Such a request is ego-based and the universe understands only the higher language of an integrated soul. Ego-based desires cannot be expressed with clarity outside of the human reality. Therefore, it seems as if you end up manifesting nothing at all.

Being unconditional means allowing the universe to comply with your request in the way it sees fit from its broader perspective. Would you turn away free pennies because they are too small, being willing to take free nickels? You might get one nickel a day, but your free pennies might add up to ten dollars a day. You will never know how abundant you could be unless you accept the pennies and see them as an expression of abundance rather than evidence of your own lack.

Being unconditional means trusting that whatever you are given has a reason or purpose in your life for now. It does not mean that you must settle for this for the rest of your life. It simply means that *right now* this is the most appropriate experience. In a moment everything might change. However, if you stop the process by refusing what you have been given, ultimately you will have closed yourself to the experience of receiving and end up with nothing.

Humans also mistakenly assume that the will of the universe (which is aligned with their higher selves) and the will of their ego conflict at times. They feel that relinquishing personal will to a higher will is akin to being powerless and therefore an undesirable state of being. However, the will of the universe (your higher self) and the will of your ego are always aligned when you are in your natural balanced state. If you perceive a conflict, it is caused by a fearful ego. Do not confuse the antics of your ego with your true state of being.

Once you have a good relationship with the ego and can help it process its fear, you will begin to see that there really is no difference between your higher will and that of your conscious personality. They begin to blend and integrate into a healthy sense of empowerment. If you perceive conflict, it is because the ego is placing a constraint on the universe, thus stopping the manifestation process from moving ahead.

SENSING UNLIMITED ABUNDANCE
(Meditation Exercise)

Close your eyes and picture the goal you defined earlier. In your mind's eye let go of how you want to see it manifest. Watch new, creative and unlimited ideas come to your mind that will be ways to fulfill your request. Use your imagination. Take a few minutes of silence while you explore these ideas.

For example, let us say that you want to create more abundance. Your definition of abundance might be that you need to create a lot of money. Let that idea go. Because you are unconditional about the goal, watch what the universe can provide for you. Suddenly you see yourself getting free plane tickets and offers to stay with friends in faraway places. You might get food from your neighbors and so on. The more you give of yourself, the more you see yourself receiving in return. There does not have to be direct

96

currency involved for you to create abundance. Let your imagination show you how you can bring abundance into your life unconditionally, without allowing the ego to tell you why you cannot. Feel the empowerment this provides you. After you finish, open your eyes.

✡   ✡   ✡

Step 3: Support the Focus

The next step means validating your whole reality as being part of the process. Your consciousness is like a vortex. It draws in ideas and processes them. Your goal is in the center of the vortex. This means that everything you draw into your life—without exception —is applicable to your goal and supports your focus, even if it seems totally unrelated.

For instance, let us say that your goal is to be a success. You are busy creating yourself as a success and suddenly you come down with the flu. You are home in bed for three days and cannot make your phone calls or do your work. You might think, "Why did this occur to interfere with my life and becoming a success?" Understand that your getting the flu is not interference, but part of the focus and the flow of your process. It supports the focus of your reality. Something is happening on the inner levels of yourself that requires this time in bed.

Every aspect of your reality supports the focus. It does this whether or not you believe it does! You might as well be conscious of this so that you will stop kicking yourself for creating such "negative" events. There is no such thing as an extraneous event. The focus is *always* supported. You might not consciously know how or why events happen as they do, but that is quite all right. If you consciously understood everything in your reality, you would be too busy figuring it all out to have any time to live! It is okay not to know. *Living* is more important.

SEEING HOW YOU ARE SUPPORTED
(Meditation Exercise)

The following is an exercise to assist you in shifting your perceptions about these seemingly extraneous events.

Make yourself comfortable and close your eyes. In the reality that you are trying to create now, find an instance that seemed to be an interference. (If there are many, then choose one.) With the understanding that all experiences support the focus, allow yourself to look at this instance of "interference." Can you see how it is related to your experience? What part can it play in the ultimate accomplishment of your goal? You do not need to find out the real reason for the distracting incident, but play with possible reasons and feel the sense of support that the universe might be extending to you. See if you can feel that this experience really did support the focus.

☼   ☼   ☼

Step 4: Allow and Trust

People might feel that this step is passive and therefore resist it. By allowing and trusting, a person might think that they are not doing anything. However, by allowing and trusting, you actually *are* doing something that is even more powerful than "trying." This step finally allows you to stop trying and to finally *be*, because you cannot "try" and "be" at the same time. Trying implies a resistance toward the outcome, so if you find yourself trying to do something, ask yourself why you are resisting the outcome. There might be a fear, or you might be trying to push in the wrong timing.

Trying is not the same as doing. Doing is very close to being. When you are being something, you automatically do it. Trying is sometimes an excuse for not doing. As you practice allowing and trusting, you must stop trying. This step demands that you know that your reality is exactly what it needs to be at any given moment.

Trusting does not mean assuming that the universe is going to give to you exactly what you want when you want it. Those are conditional desires. Trusting means that you know deep within that whatever occurs is what needs to occur, and you learn from each of those experiences. Trust in the flow, not in the manifested outcome. When you hope only for the desired outcome, disappointment ensues, because hope can imply despair. This becomes an endless cycle of disappointment in which you lose your faith in the whole process. Success must never be equated with achieving a physical outcome. Success can be measured only through what you gain on the inner levels that then create the physical world.

When you were a child it was very natural to trust your mother. Along the way perhaps your mother somehow disappointed you because she did not get you the lollipop you wanted. Soon, when your desires became very strong and were not always fulfilled by your mother, you stopped trusting her because she disappointed you.

In reality, her responsibility to you was not to give you all the lollipops you wanted, but to give you the basic needs such as love, trust, and nurturing—the inner values rather than the external frills. The same is true for your reality. Begin trusting your reality to give you the things you inherently need as a soul, such as nurturing, love and joy. These are qualities that are already present within you just waiting to burst forth. You must become willing to give these to others before you can become capable of receiving them yourself.

Here is an analogy that illustrates allowance: You are floating down a river in a canoe and the paddles are poised precariously above the water. The current is taking you quite nicely down the river, so there is no need to use the paddles. However, every once in a while you dip the oar in just to alter your course a little to avoid the rocks. If you were to stop allowing the natural flow of the river to carry you, it would be like paddling wildly, trying to force the river into submission. You only end up spinning in circles and losing your perspective of the shore. Many of you have experienced this in your life when you have gotten in your own way through inappropriate and poorly timed action. Hence the term, "Go with the flow."

The following is an exercise to assist in the process of moving with the natural currents of the universe.

LETTING GO WITH THE FLOW
(Meditation Exercise)

Once you get to that still place inside, ask yourself truthfully if you are willing to give up trying and instead embrace doing. Play with that idea. See what kind of emotional energy that idea generates. What does it mean to you to stop trying? Imagine that you have given up "trying" to reach your goal. As you are doing this, place your hands in the same positions on your body as in the earlier exercise (your right hand where you feel the fear and your left hand on the strength). Imagine your reality as you give up trying and at the same time empower yourself with the energy you are channeling through your body.

This time continue to circulate the power through your hands into your body at a rapid rate, allowing yourself to feel the power of letting go, allowing and trusting. See clearly that letting go of trying does not mean letting go of your goal. It actually moves you closer to it. Feel a new sense of empowerment within the ease of trusting and allowing. When you release the idea of trying, you open the channels within you so they can circulate more energy.

✩   ✩   ✩

Step 5: Have Patience

You might have heard the phrase, "You cannot push the river." You cannot push the river no matter how hard you row because you will capsize or spin out of control. You only cause yourself more distress if you try to push ahead. Patience is one of the biggest human challenges, because your natural state of existence is in a reality where there is no time lag between thought and manifestation. You are not accustomed to waiting for the universe to comply! If you can master this concept, your physical experience will be much more pleasurable.

Ask yourself what the concept of patience means to you. See what fears and frustrations it elicits.

If you put a cake in the oven, you have to wait for it to bake. If you keep opening the oven and slamming the door, it will not make the cake bake any faster. That illustrates the process of your own becoming. There are forces on deep inner levels that your ego does not perceive.

Things cannot move or shift in your reality until these processes are complete enough to handle the changes. By invalidating that process, you prolong your own evolution. Being patient supports the process of your own becoming. It is vital that you acknowledge this, allow it, and trust that the process is what it needs to be.

While you are practicing patience, distract yourself with fun and meaningful activities that bring joy and love into your life. Ultimately, that energy provides a wonderful oven in which your manifestations can bake to their natural, well-timed birth.

Something very beautiful and profound happens in that waiting period. If you disturb the waiting period, you will disturb the eventual outcome. If you have a soufflé in the oven, it will surely fall if you keep opening and slamming shut the oven door! If you stand by the oven for the whole twenty minutes while the cake is baking, you will see how it slowly rises and subtly changes color. If you are too impatient at having to wait, you will miss the beauty of the metamorphosis.

Patience, waiting and stillness are ancient ideas within Eastern mysticism that represent a state of being rather than an empty void. The Western world sees waiting as a void, which causes much stress and tension. Perhaps you have seen Eastern masters sit for long periods in meditation. One might think, "My goodness, how can they do this?" They can do it because they are not waiting for a void within them to be filled. They are instead *dancing in the void.*

TRANSFORMING IMPATIENCE
(Meditation Exercise)

Take yourself to that still place within. Imagine sitting beside a beautiful pond. The grass around you is green, the sky is blue, and the birds are singing. Look down at the water in front of you and see a tiny shoot pushing itself out from the pond. Focus your consciousness on this shoot so that your perception and your reality are entirely centered on this tiny green plant. Watch this shoot grow ever so gently, almost imperceptibly. You cannot actually see it moving, but you can feel or tune in to its growth so that you *feel* its birthing process. Watch a bud begin to form, at first the size of a pinhead. Marvel at the beauty of this experience.

You would not dream of pulling on the little shoot to make it grow faster. Instead, you sit patiently and watch its life unfold. The bud gets bigger and you are enthralled to watch this miracle. Nothing is more important than this. Imagine that you see a white spot of color at the tip of the bud as it begins to open. Marvel at

101

how, even though you do not see the shoot growing, you can perceive its changes. It is almost as if *you* are changing enough to enable you to see this miracle occur.

The bud gets bigger and the white begins to protrude from the tip of the bud. You see the bud bulging and the white petals lengthening. It seems as if the changes within you are developing the bud in front of your eyes. You cannot discern whether you are helping to create this or whether it is happening independent of you. It does not really matter, for your consciousness is changing as rapidly as the bud.

Now see the leaves begin to unfold. The bud is still small. As you watch, it gets larger and you know it to be a lotus blossom. The petals begin to unfold. View the complete unfoldment of this blossom to the height of its life as a lotus. Do this at your own pace. Do not rush it. Take as much time as you need to experience this profound event.

When you have created the blossom to be at the peak of its existence at the strongest potential of its life, stop the exercise and identify yourself with the blossom. Your state of consciousness has matched your experiences in this exercise just as it does when you create your reality. Your consciousness will *always* match what you are creating. It becomes one idea, one expression. Then take the blossom and place it within your heart. Whenever you feel impatient, remember this experience. There is no such thing as wasted time.

✿   ✿   ✿

Everything you experience you have *chosen* to create. It is not your ego personality who has created these experiences, but your total self, which includes your higher self. Your choices originate from a level of self far beyond that of your ego personality and extend far beyond the ego's definitions of reality.

Step 6: Bless Your Reality
and Let Go to Your Higher Purpose

As you take these steps to create your reality, your ego begins to surrender its compulsive need for control and your purpose and goals begin to align with the divine purpose quite clearly. You see that your will and divine will are exactly the same. The more you let go, trust, allow, and be the idea you want to become, the more you align yourself with the divine purpose. It cannot be any other way.

If you feel that your goal is taking too long to fulfill, then it is obvious that there is more inner work to be done. Listen to the blatant signals that reality gives you. This process does not have to be painful. It becomes painful only when you judge that you are a terrible person because your reality is not manifesting at the pace your ego deems necessary.

If you follow all of these steps energetically and emotionally, you will experience a deep inner peace about your ability to manifest. Many of the questions and frustrations you have had will dissolve as you feel your power and your connection to the universe. All it requires is that you take the first step and continue walking the path one small step at a time despite any perceived obstacles. Trust in your divine guidance. Most of all, trust in yourself.

MAKING IT HAPPEN
(Meditation Exercise

Imagine a vortex of energy around you. You are its center point. Make your goal a state of being (rather than a physical manifestation) and bring that goal into the center of the vortex. Create an emotional connection to this goal. What would it feel like to be the idea you wish to create? Within the center of this vortex let yourself feel emotionally and energetically what it would be like to become your desired state of being.

Imagine how good it would feel to become your full self. Pretend you know what it would feel like. Hold that feeling and expand it a little further by allowing yourself and your reality to be unconditional. Feel yourself flooded with light—energy from *your* universe. This represents all the different ways your reality can manifest. Feel it come into your vortex and speed it up. The energy in the vortex feels stronger because you are allowing everything the universe has to give to come into your vortex.

The vortex is spinning. Everything caught by its energy automatically supports you—even things to which you do not yet feel a connection. Feel these new things come into your spinning vortex; know they are a part of you somehow and that they are supposed to be there. Let them serve you. Feel yourself empowered by them. These seemingly extraneous ideas only empower you the more, for all support your focus.

As you stand in the center of the energy within the vortex, relax like a rag doll into it and let it support you. Allow and trust the vortex to support you, to hold you, to nurture you. As you relax, feel yourself buoyed by it. You can let go, you can allow, you can trust that this vortex you have created around you is safe. As you hold that energy, pause for a moment.

Though it feels as if there is silence within you and a storm going on around you, let that still point remain quiet while observing the beauty of the energy moving around you. Tune in to the subtleties of energy and learn from them. See clearly that there is no void, no waste of time, just conscious energy everywhere.

As you have your experience, thank yourself, bless the vortex, and send it love. Feel gratitude for all the support you have around you and send this sense of gratitude to the vortex, to God, to All That Is.

Now let go of the need to generate the vortex. As you do, at first it might wobble or spin more slowly, but it still spins. Feel the vortex moving farther away from your body. You are still at the center, you can still feel it there. Let it move outward all around you into the physical world now to begin the manifestation process.

Let yourself feel comfortable with this separation because you will attract another vortex. Watch as the vortex moves outward and dissipates. Just because you cannot see it does not mean it no longer exists. This vortex is your creation, one you have generated from within. It has now moved into the physical realms to manifest the changes you have just created. Let it do its job.

Send a golden light into the top of your head all the way down through your chakra energy centers, then out of your base chakra and into the Earth. Feel this beam of light hooked into the center of the Earth to ground you there.

◯ ◯ ◯

Continually Creating Your Destiny

This realm of physicality is where you have taken on the greatest challenges. From the greatest challenges come the greatest rewards.

Though the idea of destiny exists, it exists only as your probable path, because you always have the free will to steer your life in any direction that seems appropriate at any time. There is not just one destiny. You can create anything you wish at any time.

A destiny that you might feel deep inside usually represents a prebirth choice, one that you have chosen as a major theme in this life. As you walk the path of your life, you are given many opportunities to reinforce that choice (or so-called destiny) or veer away from that path altogether. No matter how the illusion of physical reality tells you otherwise, you are *always* the ultimate creator of your reality through the choices you make. You continually re-create your destiny with your every thought and feeling. Beliefs are a product of your thoughts and emotional experiences. They are the primary basis of your reality. With a healthy mental and emotional body, beliefs become positive tools for manifestation rather than limitations in the physical world. Changing your thoughts and emotions affects your beliefs and thus your reality itself!

9

CREATING ABUNDANCE
AND TRUE FREEDOM

Your ability to manifest a state of abundance is proportionally connected to your ability to create space within your consciousness. This is an energetic movement. Imagine that you stand in the center of your reality and that there is a circle surrounding you. Let that circle represent the space you create to hold the things you manifest from the universe. Some people have a large space around them, others a very tiny one. The size of your space indicates how much abundance you allow in your life. Of course, abundance does not necessarily refer only to money, but also love, joy and the sense of always having what you need when you need it.

Your space is automatically contracted when you hold limited beliefs. These limited beliefs might be about your own self-worth, deservability, desirability or capability. They can be acquired beliefs or programmed ones. Through your own limited beliefs about yourself, your belief system can actually contract the space around you. When your space is contracted, you feel as if you are always struggling for what you have, as if you never have enough.

When teachers attempt to help you learn to be abundant, what they are really doing is showing you how to expand your space. When your space expands, it is a result of a change in beliefs. As this happens, you open up and become less limited and constricted. You then allow more raw universal energy into your field.

When you create more space energetically, that space needs to be filled with something, otherwise your habit of constriction will emerge once again. When you work with your own internal meditations and visualize this space as something real, you can fill it with light, color and ideas that represent a sense of what you wish to create. In your imagination visualize a large room and decorate it in a way that leaves you feeling limitless. Dedicate the space by declaring, "This space is for my growth" or "This space represents my expanding abundance." This helps you to continue expanding the parameters of the space so it will never become stagnant.

If you create a space and do not fill it, it has a tendency to contract. Physical reality is created from these rather abstract understandings of the soul. These abstractions, based upon your focus and your beliefs, mold and shape themselves within physical reality as the qualities of your life.

Abundance is equal to the amount of growing space you give yourself. Your own beliefs in limitation contract the space.

When you are working with your own personal process, it becomes useful to create a metaphorical world that symbolizes what you are attempting to experience. When you do it this way, the ego feels less threatened because it is distracted by the process. The ego's defense systems, erected to protect you from new ideas and growth, then loosen their grip. When you allow yourself to both speak and receive the universal language of metaphor and archetypes, communication to and from the universe becomes much smoother.

Here is a brief technique that, when practiced on a regular basis, will truly allow you to feel more limitless and expanded inside your own space. This will assist you in manifestation and in feeling more in tune with the universal flow.

CREATING THE SPACE FOR ABUNDANCE
(Meditation Exercise)

Take yourself to your own personal quiet space through whatever meditation techniques fit you best. Once there, imagine that you are in a large room. The walls are painted white and through open windows blows a warm, comforting breeze into the room. There are no objects or furnishings in this room. It might seem sparse to you, but it feels safe. Now imagine that this room begins filling with a sparkling green energy.

You can call this energy the *green electromagnetic energy of potential*. This GEEP has the ability to expand the walls of this room as long as you allow it on all levels of your being. Feel it expand these walls in front of your inner sight.

Pay attention to how easy (or difficult) it is for you to expand these walls. This will give you an indication of your internal resistance. Expand the walls and fill the room with as much GEEP as you can. Stop when you intuitively sense the room is filled enough for now.

✿   ✿   ✿

This green energy represents the natural energy of the universe that all beings have the right to use for their own creations. There is no limit to it; it is not rationed. Thus there is no reason to hoard it. You can have as much as you need anytime you need it. Best of all, it is free, it is yours, and you can shape it into your heart's desire.

If you sense a limit to this energy or a difficulty in using it for your own creations, understand that the feelings of limitation come only from *you*. This means that further personal work needs to be done in the areas of worthiness, self-love, and deservability.

It is best to do this exercise every day and become familiar with that room, because it truly represents your inner beliefs and potentials. Over time you will see the correlation between this room and your outer physical life. You will also become more in tune with this green energy and more confident in using it for your physical life. Once you can actually become one with it, you will have succeeded in triumphing over your limited belief systems and become more of a conscious creator.

Doing this exercise without the *green electromagnetic energy of potential* would not be enough because the room must be filled lest the walls contract. Your soul and body are comprised of light, therefore light must be an active ingredient in your creations. It is the absence of light that creates contraction, so the more light you can put into the room, the more you will expand.

When you truly feel your own light, you expand as a spiritual being. Green is the fertile energy of creation. It is attuned to the frequency of your heart. Green light magnetizes your desired creations. This is understood by your unconscious because it is well-versed in the language of archetypes and symbolism.

109

Belief systems are held by more than just your conscious mind. In fact, the beliefs your conscious mind is unaware of mold your life more than you realize. You will need to do some serious inner work with your belief systems at the same time you work with the above exercise. There is not only one possible technique to work with the subconscious, but many. You will need to find techniques that are personally comfortable and powerful for you. Some of these techniques are traditionally psychotherapeutic, like Gestalt therapy, while some are considered "alternative," like hypnotherapy and rebirthing. It is not as necessary to consciously understand the belief systems that limit you as it is to simply do the processing and let the unconscious do the rest.

Also, one of the most damaging activities in which you might engage would be judging your progress. This stops the flow of energy and actually contracts your room, making it impossible to utilize the GEEP to its fullest.

Judgment is a defense mechanism that stops you from growing.

Defense mechanisms stop you from discovering your limiting beliefs. Guilt and judgment are the two most insidious manifestations of these defense mechanisms. With each layer of limiting beliefs you discover, you will also find a layer of defenses. Only when you address those defenses will you truly see your belief systems clearly.

These belief systems (and the defense mechanisms that protect them) are layered like an onion. The outer layers will be the easiest to remove because some of them are likely to be conscious. They might include past-life memories, childhood memories, or embarrassing memories of "wrong" actions you have taken and the beliefs or lessons adopted from these experiences. As you move toward the core beliefs, you move more into the unconscious realm. At that point the unconscious language archetypes and imagery become invaluable clues.

You can use the abundance exercise each time you write checks to pay bills, for example. Imagine yourself inside that space charged with the GEEP. Close your eyes for a minute and imagine the green energy filling you. Let it run down your arm into the pen and onto the check. Feel as if the check, the pen, your money and you are one complete entity. Breathe it. Be it. Write the check with all the energy of abundance you can muster. Put the check in the envelope. Seal it and stamp it. Set it aside and let it go.

Let it go! Do not attach yourself to your fear of not having enough. Send it off unconditionally. As it weaves itself into the world, it will help you create space and the energy will come back to you. You have charged that check and what it represents. It has your signature vibration on it, and the energy will eventually return home.

Financial Sovereignty

It is highly important for people to learn to become self-sufficient in whatever way they can. This is not an exercise to protect you from earth changes or a corrupt government. Self-sufficiency can create a powerful inner state of being when it is embraced from a nonfearful attitude. Self-sufficiency on inner levels of being can lead to a state of spiritual sovereignty—a state in which the source of your own power is *you*.

The more self-sufficient you become, the less strain you put on the infrastructure and institutions that most people depend on—food delivery, for instance. As you become less dependent, societal systems can go through their transformations with the least amount of drama. The more dependent you are on these systems, the more you use them out of fear and then it becomes depleted. In this case, the system cannot transform itself because it has too many dependents.

Should you wish to preserve wealth in the event of societal chaos, it is recommended that you invest in something tangible such as real estate, land, gold, silver, or other valuable commodities that can be traded or bartered during difficult times. In this case you actually receive a physical exchange for your wealth. These methods can preserve wealth in times of economic instability. When you put your wealth into tangible items, something happens inside you on a very deep level. You begin walking a road of self-empowerment because you become less dependent on an unbalanced system and its fictional definitions of wealth.

Historically, as the debt system grew through time, people came to misunderstand the meaning of value. Value has been arbitrarily altered according to the choices of the world power structure.

One paper dollar is only as valuable as the quantity of bread it can buy, and that value can change at a moment's notice. You have not, in general, experienced the meaning of stable value in your lives.

You have not had a sense of your own worth—and thus your wealth—because the money itself is simply paper. It is no longer backed by anything except empty promises. You have lost touch with the nature of value. True value represents items that can be used in a sovereign state of existence independent of the arbitrarily assigned value given by others. Such tangibles include land, which is the most valuable because it is a foundation for existence. Also valuable are metals for bartering or exchange, cloth, water, tools, the ability to create food resources, and anything else able to support a sovereign state of being.

When you begin putting your wealth into tangible items that further your growth into sovereignty, you receive a sense of the value of yourself. Internally this changes you. It frees you more and more from dependency on the system. One of the single most important issues during this time of instability and change is that you, in all levels of your life, must learn to become less dependent.

Learn to be less dependent on your mate, parents, government and economy. If you are less dependent, you lessen the strain on the whole. If you lessen the strain, the system can transform itself with milder birth pangs. This will benefit the system as well as you, and it will help you gain a sense of yourself and your abilities on a deep level that reaches far beyond the intellect. This is a very subtle yet powerful inner change from dependency to sovereignty. You will see miraculous changes in yourself—later reflected in the world—as you move toward this state of sovereignty.

These are only suggestions. Follow your intuition. If in your fear you become more dependent on the system, then you will most definitely experience chaos. The system cannot sustain too many dependents. It will burn out. To some degree that is what happened in Russia. Governments were never meant to be your parents. They were meant to protect and help you, but ultimately to be governed by you. In giving your power to the government so it would take care of you, you have disempowered yourself and created fertile ground for corruption.

Ancient texts such as the Bible talk about the evils of usury, which is the process of borrowing and lending money with interest. These texts say that usury is the beginning of a chain that leads to destruction. To some degree this is true, because once borrowing and lending become a business, the best interests of the individual are not foremost. If you can at all manage it, never borrow money at interest. If you must, consider it very carefully. The process itself is based on fictional wealth and is really a gamble. It promotes disharmony within any system. You might seem to benefit on the surface, but the underlying dynamic keeps you working longer, with less time to cultivate the fruits of freedom because you must pay the moneylenders.

A system based on individual self-responsibility can never be corrupted. The only systems that can be corrupted are those that do not promote individual freedom and have dependency interwoven into their fabric. This is why, throughout time, just about every government in the world has had some level of corruption. Governments have evolved into entities that take responsibility and sovereignty away from the people. Once that happens, the government and its people become an interdependent system incapable of freedom or higher evolution without radical change.

Governments are part of a codependent system that eventually leads to total dysfunction and collapse unless evolution begins at the grassroots level through individual evolution. Right now this grassroots evolution is occurring. It remains to be seen if it will achieve transformation before the system itself disintegrates.

Wealth has meaning only when you feel lack. It is a matter of polarity. Your true state is that of infinitely abundant beings.

Most people have not yet learned how to step into this state and let it serve them. Let us say that you could have everything you wanted whenever you wanted it. How then is wealth defined? There can be no wealth because it is only measured against a state of lack. Wealth is a measure of what you have compared to what others have—or lack.

Some extraterrestrial societies (such as on several Pleiadian planets) have a system called the *equal value system,* which is a reflection of their beliefs about abundance and the free state of their society.

The equal-value system might sound simplistic, but it actually requires tremendous spiritual and emotional evolution to master. As an analogy, if you need food in that society, you simply walk into the supermarket, get the food and leave without paying. When someone comes to you for your service, you provide it without charge. This system reflects a balance of wealth that has no arbitrary, constantly shifting values. The foundation of their wealth is a deep sense of value for each member of society. Everyone is eager to keep their world evolving by constantly following their creative excitement.

This type of planetary economy is a holistic unit. In criticizing this type of society, one might ask obvious questions such as, "Who takes out the garbage or performs the unpleasant tasks?" In a society where creative freedom is encouraged and not suppressed, there are many inventors who create technology to deal with every challenge, garbage included. Free-energy devices have been created to handle all of the planet's energy demands.

Without a government or a corporation hoarding profits and controlling new discoveries, the best interests of the society as a whole or as individuals are never overlooked. The spirit of the society is expressed through constant achievement and creative freedom rather than constant profits. This is a symptom of a healthy holistic organism. Where there is a need, there is someone to fill the need. This might sound alien to you, but look at the many enthusiastic inventors in your world who want to promote alternative fuel sources but who are stopped by big business.

Any planet can eventually develop this type of society. However, it cannot happen now on Earth while you are in the present level of fear. If one day all the world leaders said, "Okay, from now on we have the Pleiadian equal-value system," there would be chaos! There would be tremendous hoarding, because you would not believe you deserve it. You would feel as if you had to grab as much as you could before someone changed their mind. Your planet is simply not emotionally ready for this type of system. There is too much invested in lack and victimhood. There is too much invested in the polarized belief of the have and have-not mentality.

There must be a deep internal transformation before you can embrace the Pleiadian equal-value system or your own version of the equal distribution of wealth. Communism was an immature attempt at an equal-value system. So is capitalism. A true equal-value system that supports society will not have any oppressive control, rigidity or constraints attached to it. Because society is tiring of the old game of lack and wealth and you are moving toward ideas that reflect self-responsibility, a precursor to an equal-value system will appear when the time is right.

Freedom begins at the individual level. It is a concept carried deep within the soul, and when expressed through your physical lives no structure can stop its spirit. However, you must remember that freedom and equality are inherent properties of your spirit. Once recognized, you must then begin exercising your freedom, otherwise you will continue the cycle of dependence and corruption in a downward spiral.

If you become more self-responsible and affiliate yourself with others who are making the same choice, you will always have what you need when you need it. Always. It is a very different way to live. These words do not convey the true depth of the meaning of freedom of the spirit, because words always fall short in such matters. Be aware that bondage is a state of mind and a state of heart.

Choose freedom, live that freedom, and watch your lives and your planet transform before your eyes.

10

RELEASING CONFLICT AND CONTROL

Your fears must be confronted now that the shift is occurring. See your fears as challenges, for they allow you to grow by leaps and bounds. Your fears anchor you away from the flow of the mass consciousness. You who choose to pull up anchor and move with the tide might feel some initial fear, but you will quickly move through it and begin manifesting all that you want to create in life.

Confronting Your Fears

As discussed previously, your biggest fears are always connected to your biggest desires. They are opposite sides of the same coin. You must move through your fears in order to manifest your desires. You can deny your fears and never move through them, or you can choose to confront them like the spiritual warriors you can become. This will lead to self-empowerment and tremendous spiritual growth.

Get in touch with the part of you that is the spiritual warrior. This part is very powerful indeed. Begin by not only facing your fears when they appear, but by consciously invoking them. To invoke your fears, you must become inwardly vulnerable and say to the universe, "I am ready to create what I want in life. I am ready to stop allowing my fears to control my destiny."

When you begin confronting your fears you will be joining the tide of the mass consciousness. The momentum of that tide is so powerful that it cannot help but carry you downstream. As you confront those fears, you have the support and love of the mass consciousness behind you. If you continue to deny them (or never fully engage them), the probability is quite high that you will never fully manifest your potential. In that case, life will become a state of perpetual limbo that, while being tolerable, might never become what you intended when you chose to incarnate on Earth.

The energies of the closing millennium are powerful indeed. This is why many of the mystics, indigenous elders and prophets during the last few thousand years have not been able to see very far beyond this new millennium. It is not an ending, as some have theorized, but a beginning.

It is a new dawn. It is your opportunity to become the person you want to be and to create a planet of light. Recognize the great power that each of you possesses to change this reality. Just because it does not happen overnight does not mean that it isn't happening.

Trust and allowance—in combination with the willingness to confront your fears—will see you through the new millennium with ease.

Fear personifies itself within your ego, and it will play as many games as it can to keep you in fear. It plays itself out within your own consciousness, but it also manifests in the world as paranoia. For instance, there is much energy being fed to negative extraterrestrial propaganda and the supposed power the ETs have over you. This is totally distorted. The only power *any* beings have over you is through the fear they can instill in you. If you know how to integrate fear, you will not become afraid when you hear the latest fear-inducing propaganda. You will know how to remain in an empowered state.

Right now extraterrestrials are playing the role of external bogeymen. They are really just a manifestation of what is going on within all of you. You also have an internal bogeyman—Mr. Fear. The illusion is that the external fear (of negative extraterrestrials, for instance) is more threatening than the internal one. You tend to focus on the external rather than the internal reality. However, the internal serves to generate and hold the illusion created in the external reality.

Fear is very useful if you are about to be hit by a truck. It causes you to run or jump aside. When Mr. Fear saw its value and the power it had to make you react, it decided to become more valued by keeping you in constant fear and then making itself the hero by being your warning mechanism. Thus fear became indispensable. However, it was simply a trick to get you to believe in its value. It actually became less valuable, because it confused you and made it harder to discern true threats from illusory ones.

The ego believes, however irrationally, that if you are not in a state of fear, you do not care about your survival. That is a pretty powerful dynamic to break—no wonder most people are always in fear! So what happens if you do not care about your own survival? The ego believes you would not avoid death and thus it will cease to exist. The ego's biggest fear is of obliteration.

To redefine fear in your life means redefining survival. You will need to rewire the connection between fear and survival in such a way that the ego does not feel threatened. This means that you still have to place some value on Mr. Fear, if only to placate him. Mr. Fear can then relax, along with the ego, and you can go about your life unhindered by fears that are out of control.

Conflict Resolution

Fear is the source of all conflict on Earth. In your definition of conflict, there must be both a winner and a loser. During the dance of conflict, there are many layers of manipulation that occur on subtle levels. Sometimes, even after an issue appears resolved, the conflict nevertheless continues.

For example, let's say there are two children fighting over a piece of candy. They are slapping each other and wrestling. Eventually, one overpowers the other and grabs the candy. Here is an obvious winner and loser. The child who lost now stands up and says, "I didn't want that candy anyway. It causes cavities." In order to diminish the pain of loss, this child has minimized his hurt and defeat and submerged it. The child tries to fool the self into releasing the pain of loss, but the energy is stored instead. In terms of another layer of manipulating energy, it is also an attempt to diminish the other child's "win."

Competition and conflict are therefore never truly resolved, but merely change form. They are a form of manipulation for the purpose of gathering more energy. The only way to truly come to

119

balance within conflict is to release the need for superiority rather than try to uplift the self at the expense of others.

Let us now examine a possible evolution of the above conflict. After the child wins the candy, he gloats and the other cries. Emotions rise in both. Then the winning child says, "It's all right, I'll share the candy with you." The losing child, in order to punish the winner, wants to say, "I don't want any!" Instead, in this evolved scenario, he opens his heart and accepts the gift. This is actually a natural human behavior, without the learned manipulation and fear that plagues society.

There is tremendous healing when a prize is shared from the heart rather than for further manipulation. Balance is reached. This demonstrates a constructive way to end cycles of conflict. Individual conflict itself might not end for a very long time; however, the energy of each individual conflict can be healed by balancing it through sharing as in the above example. Soon cycles of conflict will no longer be perpetuated, anger and fear will heal, and society will move into balance. Despite outer appearances, society is now beginning this process.

Let us look at this from another angle. The mother comes into the room while the children are fighting and she scolds or even slaps them both. She forces them to kiss and make up, then breaks the candy in half to be shared. If this were to happen, the conflict would never heal in a natural and healthy way. There would be resentment on the part of the children because they were playing out a personal need for resolution that was never allowed completion. What occurred was *forced resolution.* In its aftermath will always be anger and repressed emotion.

You could choose to look at the above scenarios in light of the political protocols currently existing on Earth. You have an institutionalized approach that allows an authority figure to force a resolution from parties in the middle of an evolutionary process. This forced resolution does not allow that evolution, and disempowers the individuals involved.

Forced resolution never allows a natural evolution. This is why gun laws, abortion laws, and other forms of regulation will never get to the root of any problem. Laws do not allow natural resolution because they stop people from facing the consequences of their own actions in a way that is meaningful to them. Life has a way of teaching you what you need to learn if you allow it. You cannot force someone to learn a lesson. That will *never* happen. What you reap instead is control, manipulation and a perpetuation of the cycles of conflict.

Victimhood, the Ego, and the Soul

Let us differentiate the two types of victimhood: victimhood of the soul and of the ego. Through dealings with other individuals, most people are quite familiar with victimhood of the ego. This represents individuals whose primary identity is that of a victim. They are destructively self-centered and cannot truly maintain intimacy with another because they must absorb energy rather than give it. When you interact with them, it usually takes a lot of your energy to continue the relationship because you continually have to feed the individual's victim identity.

The ego's role of victim can be compared in some ways to an energy-hungry black hole. It continually needs its identity reinforced so that it can continue to spiral into itself. People who interact with victims often find themselves quickly drained because to survive, the victims are forced to pull other people's energy into their spiral. These people are easy to recognize by the draining effect they have on you.

Victimhood of the soul is a different experience. Cosmologically speaking, when you originally fragmented from the Source of all life, many of you experienced a wide range of feelings such as abandonment, fear and anger. You were not in physical bodies during this fragmentation, so the way in which these emotions were felt was very different from any human definition. From a nonphysical state emotions are not judged; they simply move through you and are released. But they leave their imprint so you can identify the emotion at a later time. In that nonphysical state emotions are not held, but experienced.

As you began the incarnational process on many worlds (especially the highly polarized worlds in the Orion system), you needed to manifest in physicality the emotions that you imprinted in your nonphysical state. This is often necessary in order to form your physical identity. When they begin building a human emotional foundation, souls often grasp some of the fleeting emotions that

121

have passed through them, using them as an anchor upon which to build their human identity and experience. Some choose joy, love or compassion; others, pain, fear or abandonment.

Initially, these patterns that you choose to solidify in order to create your identity in physicality are not very strong. They do not bind you. It is only when lifetime upon lifetime you play out the same pattern that you begin to confuse it with your identity as a soul. Once you forget that you are the original creator of your reality, you repeat old patterns because they are familiar. Some people call this a karmic pattern—an effect that has a self-created cause. You begin to believe that the old patterns are a blueprint for creation, whereas in fact, they are simply a distorted memory of your true identity. The cycle can be ended—like all so-called karmic patterns—only when you remember that the pattern is entirely self-imposed.

The Other Side of the Victimhood Coin

Those who play out victimhood of the soul are not the ones crying, "Poor me." Instead, they have an exaggerated perception of "poor you." These individuals attempt to take too much responsibility for everyone around them in an attempt to compensate for the intense experiences they had (or witnessed) in this life or past lives. They might well believe in their power to create their reality—but they also believe in their power to create *yours!* Those who carry this emotional pattern express their feelings of victimhood not through themselves, but through validating the victimhood of others.

These people continually draw to themselves individuals who want to play the role of victim. Most of their time is spent trying to fix everyone else without ever truly looking at themselves. They continually attract victims because they are not willing to see their own deep feelings of victimhood. Thus a cycle of victimhood is perpetuated that can spiral out of control. These are the people who eventually become martyrs.

If you look at personal development as layers of an onion, as you evolve you are continually peeling off layers. Victimhood of the ego is an earlier layer. Once that is peeled off—and especially if it is not fully healed—it will sometimes reveal victimhood of the soul—a deep wound that if not healed, will slow your spiritual evolution.

This type of wound requires that complete vulnerability be allowed within the self. As you work with it, you begin to realize how truly interconnected everyone is. You are never alone. This brings you right back to the time of nonphysicality, in which you adopted the emotional tool of victimhood to help you cope as you incarnated in a physical world. This realization will comfort you as you heal this wound. You will then see that you can never truly help another by giving energy to their ego identity as a victim. Upon this recognition, the healing truly begins.

Healing Victimhood

To heal this yourselves, you will first need to own your patterns of victimhood. This means recognizing it in yourself without judgment. At first this requires a constant monitoring of your behavior and feelings. You will need to be brutally honest with yourself. Keeping a written journal will help. This is not to punish yourself for such behavior, but to acknowledge its presence and channel the feelings that cause the behavior (such as fears of being alone and abandoned) into a newfound sense of open vulnerability and connectedness to all life.

During this healing process be aware of your interpersonal relationships. Do not allow yourself to play the role of victim or martyr. Equally important, do not cooperate with those around you who want you to validate their own victimhood. Do not give them energy when they attempt to reinforce their feelings of powerlessness. This might mean speaking up or simply walking away. Your actions speak loudly to your own subconscious (never mind theirs) about what is acceptable behavior in your life from that point forward.

Making choices to change your behavior (and thus your emotional state) will also change your electromagnetic field. These choices cannot be made on a whim; there must be emotion and commitment behind them. If you want to change something deeply within yourself, you must go within, experience the emotion, and let that energy stimulate a choice in your soul to make the change. Only then will your choices be solidly anchored and create actual physical and emotional changes.

Violence and Emotional Evolution

At the present time on Earth violence is evidence of a healing crisis. Long-repressed energy is releasing itself on a mass scale. This is not necessarily a permanent condition, nor is it a sign of the degeneration of society. As with all healing crises, it represents a release of darkness in an attempt to create a state of balance.

As the world heals and moves more solidly into a fourth-density reality, violence will happen less and less frequently because you will not have the need to create it. When one lives in a 4D society, there is little need to experience violence because lessons are integrated easily, fears do not dictate reality, and energy flows much more fluidly.

Within dream symbology violence will continue to manifest during your transition to 4D as a vehicle to help the self in its growth process. Violence in dreams will continue to be a useful tool because it speaks to the primal centers of your being. These are the fears that must be addressed and healed. Violence speaks to these primal fears directly, using the same force that they themselves generate.

Violence can dissipate the charge held by inner fears. In the moment they are released, you instantly become more powerful. At that point of dissipation and power your integration begins, and you must then keep the integration and healing process moving.

Many people still do not know how to process their emotions—or are afraid to. Violence is a last resort after integration has been continually denied, and a blocked person will either perpetrate or receive the violence. If you are a perpetrator, the energy is temporarily dissipated during the act, but is collected into a pool. That pool of energy must somehow be integrated. This means that the person must own it and seek healing. If it is not integrated, the cycle must continue.

If you have been the recipient of violence, the act releases deep primal energy within the self. This primal energy must be addressed and integrated. This means that the recipient must use the violent act as a window into the self in order to learn and grow. If the act is not used as a growth tool and the deep unprocessed emotion is not healed, the cycle may continue.

You can use violence consciously—through meditation and visualization—as a tool to bleed off this repressed energy in the unconscious. Native peoples knew this, and during their vision quests they allowed all visions to have free reign. In using the metaphor of violence during meditation, please be aware that it should not be used as itself but as an archetype that has its role in the healing process. Archetypal violence is never targeted at a specific person but at a part of the self that needs transformation. Since the outer reality is simply a reflection of the inner, any work within the self automatically affects your outer reality.

It is up to you to go within and find your darkness. There are many ways to confront it. You can befriend it and encourage it to reveal its vulnerability, thus building mutual trust, or you can battle it. Different situations call for different techniques. If you address your own darkness on an ongoing basis and seek healing from those exchanges, you will have no need to create violence in the outer world.

Dreams always communicate to the unconscious through archetypal imagery. If you refuse to deal with the darkness that shows up in physical life, your dream state will attempt to do it for you. Dream imagery can be very creative—you might chop up monsters, engage in battles, confront evil spirits or everything in between. Ultimately, you are reconnecting with a part of yourself and attempting to heal an imbalance.

CREATING A CAST OF CHARACTERS
(Written Exercise)

The following is suggested as a first step in your healing process. Begin to create a cast of characters for your own personal stage play. Make all these characters representative of aspects of yourself. Give them names and faces. Imagine what they look like. Draw them if you wish. Write about their unique personalities. Your cast might be composed of characters such as Mr. Fear,

125

Death, Needy Child, Authoritarian, Bad Boy, Bad Girl, Good Boy, Good Girl, Victim, Martyr and so on.

Let these characters come alive within you through your inner dialogues and daydreams. When you get to know them, they will begin to put on different costumes and appear in your dreams. You will see them appear internally during your waking hours when you are tired, stressed, or feeling insecure. If you befriend them, you will have a very clear window into the self. These aspects will become tangible to you and thus easier to confront. This provides a wonderful initiation leading to self-healing, one that will make your inner archetypal work effortless and enjoyable.

✧　　　✧　　　✧

Do not, in your visualizations, attach violent imagery to specific people because that will attach you to them and thus to the emotion itself. You have all you need within your inner tool box to use your imagery archetypally to dispel uncomfortable energies. Just use your imagination. If at any time you attach violent imagery to a specific person or people, it is time to seriously question yourself and your motivations. Most likely your intent has more to do with causing them harm than healing yourself. This would of course only lead to a downward spiral.

Natural vs. Inappropriate Anger

There is natural anger and there is inappropriate anger. If you suffer from inappropriate anger, it would serve you to find a healing modality or some therapy that will help you release the repressed emotion.

There are methods to channel anger in a healthy way. Let us say that you are driving on a freeway in Los Angeles. Someone cuts in front of you, creating a very dangerous moment. You have many options. A common response is to yell obscenities, tailgate the car or make aggressive gestures. This focuses a very tight beam of energy toward the other person. But because you live in a reflective universe, *all energy you put out returns to you*. Therefore this tight beam of energy will eventually return. The cycle of give and take never ends.

Let us say that instead of focusing the energy in such a tight beam, you release your anger in a dissipative way—you might pound the steering wheel, scream, or breathe heavily. You are releasing the energy but not directing it at the other person. You remember that they are really just a reflection of you. If you do it this way, your energy will not return to you in a tight, uncomfortable beam; instead, you will simply absorb your undirected anger.

Please remember that you *always* cocreate your reality with whomever you are interacting and that *you alone entirely create your reaction* through your own choices. Because each person is a teacher, you can learn a lot from those who trigger your anger. What you learn can help you become a healthier and more self-empowered person. To blame another person is the same thing as cutting off your own right arm, proverbially speaking.

The people in your reality with whom you are angry are only physicalized symbols of an anger that is sourced from deep within the self. If you lose your temper every time the neighbor cuts his grass or the mailman is late, it is a sure indication that although these people might seem to be the targets of your anger, they are certainly not the cause.

Anger always boils down to an anger at the self (even if it appears as an anger toward God). This anger might express feelings of not being good enough, smart enough, popular enough or powerful enough to have your life under control. You might be angry that you have allowed someone to abuse you. Underneath the ego constructs, the soul can still feel anger. If you remove all ego constructs such as blame, shame and guilt, you might find that the higher personality is really angry at the reality it has created! The difference between the ego and the higher personality is that the ego blames others outside of itself, whereas the higher personality is aware that it alone is the creator of its experiences, and it takes responsibility for its own creations.

This is where transformation occurs. When you realize that you are the creator of your experiences, you then learn to take appropriate action—not based upon blaming another. Anger is truly an emotion that can pass through you very quickly once you learn how to release it in a nondirected way.

In physicality, anger channels through the lower-body energy centers. As a whole, individuals who carry a lot of anger have digestive and/or reproductive problems. The unreleased energy is being held there. The Earth herself can serve as a wonderful absorber of energy if you allow her to help you. Anger is meant to be released through all of the lower chakras and into the Earth. The Earth transmutes and recycles this energy, feeding it back to you in a healthy way. Physical movement such as walking, running or biking helps release energy and grounds you into the Earth.

Human-centered activities are equally important to your spiritual evolution. True evolution is gained through a balance of the physical and nonphysical realities. The feeling and releasing of healthy emotion must be integrated with spiritual pursuits of your choice such as meditation, yoga and so on. Without that balance you do not develop as an integrated and healthy spiritual human being.

Remember, you chose to be physical. Rolling in the mud or having sex does not make you any less spiritual!

INTIMACY AND THE SACRED MARRIAGE

The term *sacred marriage* has been used in esoteric traditions throughout the world for many thousands of years. It has several different meanings. Sacred marriage can refer to a sacred union between a man and a woman or to the unification of the male and the female energy within a person. The difference between a sacred marriage and a traditional marriage is the recognition by both parties that both the man and the woman are reflections of each other and work as partners for their mutual growth. They always see themselves reflected in each other's eyes. *A sacred marriage is a union in which the divine reveals itself through the soul of the other and the self views its own divinity in this reflection.*

A sacred marriage can also refer to the union of the physical self with the higher self. This is an ultimate goal for you on this physical plane. When you join with your divine self and become a version of your higher self here in the physical, it can be called a sacred marriage. A sacred marriage also represents your journey toward reunification with God. Sacred marriage means a unification and integration with the divine aspects of self.

Most humans are on a quest. They are searching for a mate with whom they can experience the joys of being human. When you interact with a mate, it is a way to experience a sacred marriage within yourself. The following will primarily focus on the integration and unification of the inner male and female energies. They will be deeply explored to help you tap into your inner male and female.

As male and female energy is discussed, please be aware that certain generalities—and polarized terms—must be used. Keep in mind also that each physical gender possesses both aspects and that as the evolutionary process continues on Earth, the sharp boundaries that once existed between the genders will become less defined.

Male and Female Energies

Let us first explore the human energy field and how the male and female energies are utilized. The human body has seven primary energy centers called chakras. There are other energy centers on higher spiritual levels, but for now only those related to physicality will be explored.

To recapitulate, the first chakra at the base of the spine corresponds to the color red. It relates to the basic needs of life and grounding yourself here on the Earth plane. The second chakra, located below the navel, corresponds to the color orange. This is an emotional center for the body and also the center of sexuality. The solar plexus chakra, below the rib cage, corresponds with the color yellow and governs your ability to create action and manifestation in the physical plane. The heart chakra corresponds to the color green and governs your ability to give and receive personal and universal love. The throat chakra relates to the color blue and governs your ability to communicate. The third eye chakra corresponds to the color indigo and governs your inner sight and intuition. Finally, the crown chakra at the top of your head, corresponding with the color violet, reflects your connection to God and the universe of which you are a part.

Certain chakras demonstrate primarily male energy and others female energy. The inward flow of energy reflects the female principle, because female energy is receptive. Whenever energy flows outward, it reflects the masculine principle because male energy is related to action. Each chakra processes energy differently. Three of the chakras are neither male- nor female-dominant but contain both energies. These are the base, heart and crown chakras.

The primarily female chakras are the second chakra and the third eye. The primarily male chakras are the solar plexus and throat. (This has to do with how the energy flows in and out of the body, so not become attached to the labels.) Men and women contain both types of chakra energy, but the energy flows differently in the body, depending upon one's gender.

Emotion is energy in motion. Inasmuch as the emotional structures of men and women are very different, energy flows in their bodies differently. Men and women have such different needs and such different energy fields that sometimes people have used the metaphor that they are from different planets. Many who have friends or lovers of the opposite sex might think they cannot possibly ever understand them. One reason is that the flow of energy is so different.

In the woman, the female chakra energies are connected, the second chakra to the third eye. The **second chakra** represents the area of the womb where she receives energy. This is the seat of female emotion; at certain times of the month or during pregnancy a woman's emotions become magnified. Each chakra has certain needs or desires that must be fulfilled for balance.

In a woman the second chakra always wants to absorb love and emotion. When groups of women are together, they naturally feed this to each other because they understand the other's needs. When women are with men, the men often do not know how to give her the needed energy. Because of their different needs, men are often confused about how to meet the needs of a woman. Therefore conflict arises.

The **third eye chakra** is also one where energy flows inward, resulting in the general belief that women are more intuitive than men. Women continually gather data from their environment, but not always through the eyes. It often comes through intuition. A woman is naturally more sensitive to the emotions of others. Because of the link between the second chakra (emotion) and the third eye (intuition), the female is in tune with other people's emotions. This is necessary because in rearing children they must be emotionally responsive to the child. It is difficult for many men to understand why women are so emotional, but emotion is the window through which females see the world. Therefore, the kind of love a woman responds to is what people have called a romantic or emotional form of love.

Because men and women possess both energies, what is being said about women is also true for the female side of men. However, unless a man is in close touch with his own feminine energy, this

131

female circuit might not make sense to him. All males possess this female circuit as a secondary process, but in some males it might be dominant.

The **solar plexus chakra**, primarily male, is the chakra of action and manifestation. This is why men are generally so action-oriented. History, which records events and is thus a record of actions, is a record of male achievements, of solar plexus chakra activities.

The stereotype is that women prefer romance whereas men prefer sex. This stereotype is really saying that the energy of the two is different: Women are focused in emotion and men are focused in action. Emotion is translated as romance and intimacy. Action is the sex act itself (or its pursuit). Both men and women are looking for the same ultimate fulfillment; however, they seek it in different ways. This is not good or bad, it is simply a reflection of the different energy in male and female bodies. Depending upon the individual, a man or woman might play out either a male- or female-dominated scenario.

The **throat chakra**, the other male-energy chakra, represents communication (an outward flow of energy) just as the solar plexus in its action form is an outward flow. Men are usually more comfortable communicating intellectual information than that with more emotional content. (Don't forget that both genders can display these male- and female-energy characteristics.)

All beings have a basic need to communicate love. The way a person communicates love outwardly depends on how their energy is channeled through their chakras. Men (or people with strong male energy) will communicate love through action, not emotion. In a love relationship men tend to communicate their love through sex as well other actions (such as fixing the car) for the loved one. This is natural for them. It is at this point that misunderstandings arise. Females do not need the sex act alone, but emotional fulfillment. If they do not receive it they become resentful. They do not understand that in fact, love is what they are being given. They do not understand the package in which the love is wrapped. If clear communication is not established between female- and male-dominant people, a breakdown of the relationship begins.

Once you understand what male and female needs are, it becomes much easier to come together in a clear communication and sharing of love. Ultimately, everyone has both female and male needs and must learn to balance these needs within themselves.

Three chakras utilize male and female energy fairly equally. (This is a generality, because individuals use energy differently.) **Heart chakra:** Both men and women have a basic need for heart energy in the form of love. **Base chakra:** Both genders have a basic need for grounding, sex, and/or procreation. **Crown chakra:** The basic need is for higher union. In an ideal love relationship both partners have some basic needs in common. Besides love, sex and/or procreation, ultimately they want a higher union. This is the union of the sacred marriage.

The Desire for a Higher Union

From the point of view of the soul, humans want to reunify with God. Since each person is a reflection of God, one way to create that union is through relationships.

This idea is applicable to nonsexual relationships. Let's say that you have a very close friend of either sex. There is a mutual foundational need to share love. If it is a nonsexual relationship, then the need for joint creation or creativity takes the place of sex.

The most intense energy in a friendship is often felt when you both have new ideas and get excited about doing something together. That is an example of using the energy of the base chakra. When you interact with any friend, the higher purpose is union with God. As you love each other you learn to see yourself in the other person. Once you can see yourself in everyone else, you begin the path of unification with God.

Definitions of love have been pondered since time began. Beginning with an ideal, love means seeing yourself in another person and learning to love yourself through what you see in that other person. Ultimately, love has nothing to do with another person and everything to do with yourself. If you focus on the other person at the expense of your own growth, it is not true love. When you are attempting to be your true self, you can give your love more fully to someone else.

Humans have defined love in a compartmentalized fashion. There is love with sex, love without sex, love between parents and children, and love between siblings. But love is simply one idea! The basic idea is that love is a frequency that leads to total vulnerability. When you can metaphorically undress yourself and stand naked before another person, you are giving that person the greatest gift of love possible—your real self, without barriers.

It does not matter whether or not love is sexual. Your ability to be vulnerable with someone and be your true self with that person *is* an act of love. You can do that with anyone—whether lover, friend, family member or a stranger on the street. Love is an elusive concept in your world. The irony is that everything you see is made from love.

As mentioned earlier, this love frequency is an actual expression of the universal language of geometry. You contain the frequency of the golden mean spiral within you as much as you are contained within it. It is the cosmic heart—the frequency that binds you together. No matter how much you deny love, you cannot escape your own origins. You will always seek love (even while being mired in darkness). Love is the way home.

Integrating the Inner Male and Female

Because the planet is quickly accelerating and a species evolution is occurring, you will begin awakening the male and female within you. Human males who are sensitive to these transformational changes are already beginning to get in touch with their female sides. As they do this they become more balanced, more able to communicate with women and express and love their inner female energy.

The same can be said for women who are getting in touch with their masculinity. Through that exploration they are able to communicate better with the men in their lives. Some women, however, believe that coming more into balance means denying their emotions. If a woman is repressing her emotions, it does not mean that she is getting more in touch with her masculine side! When one represses one's emotions, emotion does not go away, but gets pushed deeper into the body. Repressed emotion causes much inner turmoil and pain. It crystallizes inside the body, causes blocks, and can eventually cause disease. Healthy emotional expression is essential for the integration of the male and female energies.

Let us use an example of a healthy woman who is getting more in touch with her male energy—for example, a woman who has a high-powered career. A healthy woman in touch with her masculine energy puts a lot of energy into her career and is not afraid to take action to advance herself. She makes a decision about what she wants, makes a plan, and then accomplishes it. She can do this while still having her emotional female side. The primary way for any woman to get in touch with the male energy is to *take more healthy action* in her life.

As males and females begin evolving, females are going to become more action-oriented while still expressing their emotions. Men, on the other hand, will become less action-oriented, but more in touch with their feelings. Eventually, both males and females will meet in the middle, attaining a new compatibility because of their balanced emotional states. Please remember that all of you are healing yourselves from thousands of years of cultural conditioning regarding male and female roles. You are accomplishing a lot in a short time.

Viewed from the outside, it might seem as if men are becoming soft and women are becoming hard. That perspective comes from the old way of seeing the roles, not liking any change. A balance will eventually be reached.

Here is an exercise tool to help you integrate your inner male and female energies. You have an archetypal male and female energy within you whatever your physical gender. Your soul is neither male nor female. When you are born here you choose a male or female body, but both energies are present all the time. A simple way to connect with your male and female energies is to create images of them in your mind.

INTEGRATING THE INNER MALE AND FEMALE
(Meditation Exercise)

Do not underestimate the power of the following exercise. If you are observant, it will teach you a lot about yourself as well as help integrate two powerful forces within you. This exercise is for both men and women, and begins with the **Inner Male**.

135

Close your eyes. Imagine that you are building a man. Create this man from scratch. In your mind see the perfect male image of yourself. If you are a man, he might look somewhat like you if you wish, but make some changes so that you feel he is even more of a "perfect" man—the man you would like to become physically, emotionally and spiritually. If you are a woman, create this man to be attractive to you, but remember that he is a part of you and he represents the male version of you. Make him as masculine as you can, but do not create the stereotypically unbalanced masculine image. Create the perfectly balanced man. Once you imagine him, give him a name that is not yours.

Put this man to the back of your mind for a moment. Now begin creating your **Inner Female**. If you are female in this life, she can look like you, but make her more of whom you wish to become physically, emotionally and spiritually. If you are a man, make this inner female attractive to you, but remember that she is a part of you. Give her a name that is not yours so that she becomes real.

Clear your mind. Remember the names you have chosen for these inner male and female selves. In order to continue a relationship with them, it is essential that you actually talk to them in your mind. Make them very real. They are your companions.

Now that you have introduced yourself to these characters, it is time to complete the visualization. Make yourself comfortable, either sitting or lying down. When you are ready, close your eyes and take some deep breaths. Use your own methods to get to that peaceful place inside.

Imagine a cave. From the mouth of the cave shines a beautiful golden white light. As you walk into the cave, it is very bright but it does not hurt your eyes. Go to the back of the cave, where there is a beautiful, ornate mirror. Walk up to it and see your reflection. Notice how you are glowing with light. As you watch this reflection, consciously change it into the image of your inner male. (No matter whether you are a man or woman, try to create your inner male as clearly as you possibly can.) Look him in the eyes. Take a few minutes to dialogue with him. He might have things to tell you or you might have questions you want to ask him. He is here to help you. Make friends with this inner male, call him by his

136

name. See what he has to teach you. Feel the deep exchange of love between you.

The mirror momentarily becomes foggy. When it clears, you see your own physical reflection. Watch as this reflection changes into the image of your inner female. Call her by her name. Make a connection with her. Have a conversation with her. What does she have to teach you? Feel the love between you.

The mirror becomes foggy again and when it clears you see that your inner male and your inner female are standing together holding hands. They reach their free hands out of the mirror. You take their hands and the three of you now hold hands. They are still in the mirror and you are standing before it. Ask your spirit guides and higher self to do any necessary energy adjustments so you can begin the process of integrating the inner male and female energies. Release their hands now and leave the cave the way you entered.

✧   ✧   ✧

The Value of Separation

Here is a story of creation told from a different perspective. Once upon a time there was only one being called God. God was totally unified. God thought, "What would it be like not to be so unified? What would it be like if I didn't know myself?" God then decided to explore the idea of separation from itself. From that thought fragmentation occurred.

Metaphorically, pieces of God flew in many different directions. Even though all of these little pieces of God were separated from the whole, they were still God. Since God is a unified being, these little pieces of God always had the drive toward reunification. After they fragmented and were separate for a while, they forgot what it was like to be a whole and integrated being.

These individual pieces of God tried to understand their predicament. They were torn between two different understandings. One understanding was that God wanted them to experience separation in order to understand themselves. Therefore, these souls that fragmented from God had a drive to maintain separation and understand that state of existence. They felt they must maintain separation until the mission was completed. The second understanding was that because all of these pieces of God were still part of God, they would always be drawn toward reunification. This seemed like a paradox. How could these pieces experience the value of separation while struggling with a deep-seated desire to reunify?

All of you are these pieces of God. You have within you the urge to stay separate as well as the drive to reunify. For many humans, this apparent conflict wages an inner war. This is the root of what you have come to know as the struggle between good and evil or light and dark. If you search deep within, you can find those two drives coexisting side by side. You can sense the joy of reunification, but you can also sense the joy of becoming a separate, autonomous being. While you are here in a physical body, there is a limitation of your ability to reunify. The very fact that you have a physical body means that you are supposed to be here experiencing separation.

How then do you embrace this separation and still balance the desire to reunify with God? This is primarily accomplished through relationships. When two pieces of God come together in relationship, the natural tendency is to want to unify, yet you struggle with the desire to individuate. This polarity (and seeming paradox) is the basic foundation of life in 3D. Relationships are an opportunity to make peace with this inner battle. However, the key to keeping that peace is through the heart.

The Secret of Intimacy

The sacred marriage celebrates the reunification with God. You can express this marriage within your own internal energy or through your relationships in the outer world. However, for this union to truly take place, there is one very important ingredient: intimacy.

Intimacy means dissolving barriers. These barriers might lie between you and another soul or between aspects of the self. The ultimate intimacy was when you were merged with God in a state of wholeness. You believe you are not merged with God in that way any longer because of the nature of your physical existence. Here in the physical plane you are left with the challenge of *re-creating that original divine intimacy through your physical and emotional bodies.*

Intimacy can be expressed in many different forms. One is through emotion. Many people have a deep emotional intimacy with their friends, lovers and family. Emotional intimacy means letting someone into yourself—your light self as well as your dark self. It means letting them see your *true* self. This can be a very frightening experience for humans.

This fear might be expressed by the image of yourself totally naked standing in the front of a room full of people while everyone scrutinized you. That is a frightening thought! Emotional intimacy is just as frightening for many people. However, the paradox is that unless you totally open yourself to another, warts and all, you cannot ever be loved fully, only the parts you dare to reveal. And you will always be aware of that.

Another expression of intimacy is through the act of physical love or sex. Sex can be an attempt at divine union. Perhaps some of you have had very spiritual experiences when you have been physically intimate with someone and it made you feel like you were closer to God. This is the basic premise of tantric practices, which teach you to become vulnerable with another person so that together you can reach God. The act of physical union means that you *must* be intimate—no matter how you try to fool yourself or your partner.

Remember that in order to fulfill God's desire to experience separation, you believed that you had to keep yourselves separate because you had to experience it fully. Throughout time you devised ways to keep yourselves separate from each other. The human ego has been the orchestrator of the plan and has helped to keep you focused on separation for millennia.

Whenever your ego says to you, "I cannot open to this person. I am not good enough" or "They won't love me" or "That person is more knowledgeable than me," you are playing ego games. These games keep you separate. The ego is doing a wonderful job, but your soul desires unification. This is why you feel such conflict. You want to open to other people, but the ego will not allow it.

Each time your ego plays the game of separation, it forms blocks in your energy field and in your emotional body. It is almost like a wall that exists around you. This wall is built by all of your doubt about yourself and the ego games that keep you from loving yourself. When two people wish to begin a relationship they must first dissolve these walls before they can ever truly connect.

In a new relationship these walls show themselves through your feelings of insecurity and fear. Because dissolving the walls seems like such a life-threatening task to the ego, most people try to build relationships while keeping the walls intact. They do not know how to journey deeply into intimacy. With the walls intact, the relationship is then filled with conflict and you never truly know each other. This is not true intimacy.

In order to create true intimacy that can lead to unity, you must begin to remove the bricks and dismantle the wall. To do this, show the other person your vulnerable self—your fears, insecurities and so on. Show your partner your secret desires and positive qualities as well as your fears and darker aspects. Do not hide from each other. When you do this, you remove some of the bricks. As the bricks are removed, light starts shining through. This is when your God-self and the God-self of the other person can truly connect. A true sacred marriage can occur because you begin to see God in the other person.

The way to begin removing bricks from the wall is different for each person, but it does require communication. You must create a safe space so that you and your partner can feel comfortable being naked (so to speak) with each other. This process might be difficult for some, but truly rewarding.

Let's say a man and a woman wish to create a unified intimate space. Because of the gender differences, their energies are different, they communicate differently and have different needs. How do you create an intimate space when it is as if you are talking to an alien from another planet? Here are some basic ideas to understand.

Male and Female Needs

First, let us explore how males and females process emotion. These are generalizations for the purpose of illustration. When women are feeling emotional and do not know what they are feeling, they must talk about it, because talking helps clarify their feelings. This pattern drives males crazy. Many arguments begin at this point because fundamental needs of both parties are not understood.

When a person is feeling emotional and processing female energy, he or she might need to talk. This person only needs someone to *listen*, not do anything to fix the problem. If the receiver is focused in the male energy, he or she will be uncomfortable because they are action-oriented and will feel the need to fix the problem rather than just be emotionally present. More than anything else, the emotions expressed by the talker need to be validated simply by the listener being present and listening.

Do not assume that those who are more masculine-focused in their energy have the same needs for verbal communication. When a man is feeling emotional, he doesn't necessarily want to talk. The male emotions are not connected with speech. Often a male-oriented person will want to be left alone to process in his or her own way. The more you try to get that person to talk, the worse he or she will feel.

If you are trying to help a male-oriented person, give them silence, peace and space. This is a difficult task for someone with female-oriented emotions because it will trigger feelings of abadonment. The person trying to help begins to doubt that he or she is loved when the other person wants to get away and be alone. The irony is that the more the female gives the male space and solitude to process, the more they are in fact loved and valued on their own terms!

Part of the path toward reunification is recognizing the differences between male and female energy needs. If you can honor the needs of those around you, your relationships will become powerful and solid. You will feel a powerful state of intimacy.

Do not forget that everyone has both male and female energy. Go within and be aware of your needs and do not be afraid to express them. If both the male and the female in you feel fulfilled, something very wonderful results—*passion*. This can mean sexual passion, but it does not have to. In a nonsexual way, passion might mean excitement and zest for life. Passion means becoming excited about your connection to the universe. It leads you on the road toward integration and the ultimate sacred marriage.

Passion and unification do not mean that you must spend every moment together with a lover physically. In fact, when you are truly in love and passion exists, your time apart can be wonderful, because you always sense deeply the presence of the other. The goal here is for all of you to become *whole* beings—both inner male and inner female in a balanced way. As whole beings your relationships become more fulfilling. You might chose to live separately, be married or manifest the relationship in any way you desire. What really counts is the emotion, the vulnerability and the intimacy between you.

There are many schools of thought about monogamy. Some people believe that you can physically love more than one person at the same time and that this should be the ideal. Some people believe you can love only one person this way. To clarify this dilemma, the ultimate experience of becoming one with God is the achieving of intimacy—most especially emotional intimacy. This means recognizing the other person as an aspect of yourself. Since you are truly unified anyway, you all have the capacity to be emotionally intimate with every other person on the planet.

It is your choice as to how you manifest emotional intimacy once you are able to achieve it. Sexual intimacy can be an extension of emotional intimacy, but it does not have to be. All emotionally intimate relationships do not have to become sexual to lead to the divine self.

Humans fear true intimacy. If humans had no fear of it, the structure of your personal relationships would be unrecognizable compared to what they are now. Imagine a society that was so comfortable and intimate with each other that there could be no secrets. The very fabric of society would have to change. Honesty and integrity would become key elements openly practiced in all interpersonal relationships.

The sexual practices and preferences of individuals never hinder the path to spiritual enlightenment. There is no universal morality! Your sexuality is a reflection of what is within and of your ability for true intimacy. Sex is never the real issue. Your only true responsibility is to live with integrity and honesty and take responsibility for your actions. Some people who are considered holy are celibate. If you look closely at all the different traditions on Earth, you will see a huge variation in beliefs in sexual practices.

In one of the major contemporary Christian traditions the leaders are celibate. However, if you look at some of the tantric practices of the East, their most advanced masters are not celibate. Spiritual masters or priests might choose one mate, no mates or many mates. There is no one answer, for a very important reason: Each and every one of you has the responsibility to discover what works for you. What brings you closer to intimacy and therefore to God?

Remember that you are both a physical and a spiritual being. A physical being has needs and so does the soul. By denying either one or the other, you do not become whole. You must learn to balance the two. Anytime you repress or deny a part of yourself, you are not on a road to wholeness. Remember that *anything* can be misused: Some people use sex to achieve a high level of consciousness, and some people use sex for extremely negative purposes. What really counts are your intentions and your journey toward intimacy.

INTEGRATIVE BREATHING TECHNIQUE
(Exercise)

This is an ancient breathing technique from Lemuria, where it was used to help integrate the inner male and female energies. It will also help loosen blocks in either your male or female aspects. Begin very gently. If it is something you enjoy and that you feel works for you, eventually you might practice more aggressively which will mean much more profound results.

This technique is a way for the breath to follow the natural rhythm of energy in the body. Begin by sitting with your spine straight. If you begin to feel dizzy or lightheaded while doing this exercise, simply slow down. This will change the way energy flows in your body. For some people it can be subtle, for others, strong.

Female Energy: The female energy breath is first. Block your right nostril by pressing it closed with your finger. Open your mouth slightly. Breathe in as deeply and slowly as you can through your left nostril. Once you feel your lungs are totally filled, slowly exhale through your mouth. Don't blow it out forcefully. Exhale very gently. After you have exhaled, repeat the process. Inhale through the left nostril, gently and slowly.

While you are doing this, keep the image in your mind of the female self in the mirror that you created in the earlier exercise. This breathing technique will activate her. You might lose track of what you are doing and travel an inner journey. This is quite all right. However, try to follow the exercise as closely as possible with your eyes closed. Do this for about five minutes and then move on to the male energy activation.

Male Energy: To activate the male energy, block your left nostril by pressing it closed with your finger. Breathe in through your mouth and out through the right nostril. When you exhale from the right nostril, make the exhalation strong but not too forceful. Repeat the process. As you are doing this, hold the image in your mind of the inner male that you saw in the mirror from the earlier exercise. Continue this phase of the breathing exercise for about five minutes as above.

Integrating the Male and Female: Now combine the two breathing exercises. This will integrate the inner male and female. Begin with the female. Close the right nostril. Breathe in through the left nostril gently. Exhale gently through the mouth. Inhale through the mouth. Block the left nostril and exhale through the right nostril. Begin again by blocking the right nostril and continuing the process. While you are doing this, place the image in your mind of both your inner male and your inner female. See them holding hands.

This will become easier with practice. Once you feel confident in the process, begin the next set of instructions to complete the visualization while continuing the breathing.

COMPLETING THE INTEGRATION
(Meditation Exercise)

While continuing the Lemurian breathing exercise, use your own personal process to take you to your internal quiet space. Visualize the cave you entered earlier. Walk into the back of the cave and to the mirror. Look at your reflection. As you watch, consciously create your reflection to become your inner female self. See her as clearly as you can. From her heart comes a beautiful pink beam of energy that travels through the mirror and connects with your heart chakra. Feel your heart open to this beam of energy. Allow yourself to feel great love for this female entity in the mirror.

This female entity moves to the side of the mirror. As she does, you see your own reflection standing next to her. Watch this reflection of yourself and consciously create it to become your inner male self. See them as clearly as you can. From the heart of the inner male a beautiful green beam of energy comes through the mirror and is absorbed into your heart chakra. You are connected to the inner male by this green beam of energy. Open your heart and receive this energy. Allow yourself much love for this male entity.

Now you can see the inner female move back into the mirror so that she and the male are standing side by side. You are connected to the female by a pink beam of energy and to the male by a green beam. Place your hands on the mirror. The mirror becomes an interdimensional doorway. You can easily walk forward into it. As you do, it feels like you are entering another reality. You now stand in the realm of your inner male and your inner female.

Look at your inner female and greet her by name. She opens her arms. Allow yourself to walk into her embrace. Return her embrace and feel her love strongly. Feel her presence within you. Look now to your male self. Greet him by name. He opens his arms to you. Allow yourself to walk into his embrace and return his love. Allow him totally inside you. Feel his profound love.

Continue to practice the breathing exercise. You, your inner male and your inner female are blended together. Feel them both within you. Feel their love. Feel the strength that they give you. It is very important that you nurture this relationship with your inner male and female. Always acknowledge their presence. Always send them love. They will support you in your physical life here on Earth. They will guide you on the path of the sacred marriage.

After you feel that you are finished with your communion, step out of the mirror and back into the cave. Even when you step out of their reality, you can still feel their presence strongly. You are not alone in the cave; someone else is there. A beautiful lightbeing shines brilliantly with white light. This is your higher self. Your higher self is celebrating the marriage you have just consecrated. Your higher self has a present for you. Open your hands and receive the gift. It then opens its arms and you step into his/her embrace. Feel the light of your higher self deeply within you, for he/she too is being absorbed within you and making you strong.

There you stand within the cave filled with the energy of your male, your female and your higher self. Make a commitment to come back to Earth and live as an integrated being to the best of your ability. Take the gift from your higher self and walk out of the cave. Celebrate the marriage that you have just experienced. Conclude the breathing exercise. Slowly feel your consciousness come back to the room. Sit quietly because you will be in an altered state for some minutes.

✦   ✦   ✦

Do the breathing exercise as often as you can, especially when you are feeling stressed or blocked. It will help to balance you and move emotions through. As you become more confident with the exercise, you can allow the breaths to become deeper and stronger.

For two days following the first time you do this exercise, you might feel very different. If you feel strange energy sensations in your body, do not be concerned. Treat yourself well during those two days. Drink lots of pure water, eat well and try to stay as peaceful and calm as you can. You have just begun two powerful relationships that will be with you always. These relationships will lead you back into wholeness.

12

CREATING HEALTHY
RELATIONSHIPS

Many people are feeling a sense of urgency about letting go of issues they have carried for quite some time. These issues might have to with love relationships, family, friends, or the self. This feeling of urgency is because you are moving from one vibrational reality to another. The set of beliefs and premises that were operating in one reality *cannot* be sustained in the next. If you attempt to carry the premises and beliefs that sustain separation into a 4D reality and refuse to let them go, you can feel torn apart emotionally.

From an evolutionary perspective, the 3D premises, based on the concept of separation, were necessary for human development. They provided fundamental lessons for humans to grow through relationships. As humans evolve, so must the structure of their relationships. To illustrate the current and future evolution of relationship, let us first examine the separative principles of third density.

Principles of Third-Density Relationships

Secrecy has been a widespread manifestation. Secrecy is a withholding of information from a partner or from aspects of yourself. Secrecy does not operate only on the level of your inter-actions with others; it keeps you separated from the greater portion of yourself as well. The issue of secrecy has been very important in maintaining relationships in 3D reality, because it is an expression of separation. Many people have even felt that their ability to keep secrets is the glue that holds their relationships together!

Fear-based Monogamy. Another expression of separation is through fear-based monogamy rather than monogamy by choice. The unconscious belief is that if you can get someone to commit only to you, then you can use the relationship as a way to stop growing rather than a way to look deeply into yourself. You can thereby create an illusion of safety, separate and safe from the rest of the world. Without a means for growth, this situation usually creates unhappy or destructive relationships.

Conditional Love. Conditional love has been an expression vital to maintaining 3D relationships. Conditional love means that you will love someone only if they fulfill your needs or desires. If they do not fulfill those conditions, then you are justified in withdrawing your love. There has been a misunderstanding in 3D reality regarding the meaning of unconditional love. When you are dealing from a separative framework, the only way you can view anything is through that framework of separation. Love in 3D, therefore, is love based upon conditions.

Expectations. Humans entering into a relationship with someone have expectations that are unknowingly projected upon the partner. Even if the partner is incapable or unwilling, there still might be an attempt to force the partner to fulfill these expectations. The partner is used as a means to satisfy one's unconscious needs.

Manipulation can be covert. In the classic 3D relationship a number of deep-seated manipulations are in place so that each person's needs get filled and so each person is protected from his/her fears and feelings of lack or insecurity. These include the largely unconscious bargains that are struck for mutual protection.

The need to control is another quality inherent in solidly anchored 3D relationships. This is a mistrust of a higher reality —a mistrust that everything is happening the way it needs to for the greater good. Instead of trusting, you shape, force and mold the relationship because you do not trust that it will naturally be what it needs to be.

Since fourth density is based upon integration, the characteristics normal for 3D relationships can no longer be sustained. The qualities inherent in 4D relationships are as follows:

Principles of Fourth-Density Relationships

Honesty. Partners in a relationship must practice honesty instead of secrecy at all costs. If you see in your friend or partner that they are doing something sabotaging to themselves or the relationship, you must speak that observation *from the heart.* In 3D these perceptions are often withheld to avoid hurting the other person's feelings or to keep control of the relationship. If you are the person to whom these observations are being said, you must remember (and trust) that they are spoken *from the heart* and not react defensively. Listening to what is being said does not mean that you have to agree. Simply use the information to go within and better yourself.

Secrecy is used as a control mechanism in relationships. When honesty is accepted as a control factor, impersonal truth rather than personal control is sought. Be aware, however, that if you are using honesty as a control mechanism, then you are not speaking from your heart and your ulterior motive makes you dishonest!

It cannot be stressed enough how fundamental honesty is in a 4D relationship. If there is no honesty, the relationship cannot exist in the 4D model. It is that crucial.

This is also about honesty with the self. At times you keep secrets from yourself in order to feel safe. In a 4D reality it is difficult to keep truth from the self. You could wake up one morning and suddenly realize that the relationship you are in no longer serves you. That realization must be recognized and honored for the flow to continue. Do not bury it. If you do, you will end up perpetuating a 3D relationship that will be draining instead of nurturing. If you choose to ignore your realization, then in the long run you are not truly serving your partner.

Unconditional Love. Third-density relationships are based upon conditional love and fourth-density relationships upon unconditional love. At every moment in life everyone has the ability to experience more unconditional love than before, for it has no limit. You will need to build your own definitions because it can be conceived of only by experiencing it. Definitions are useful, but they are also intellectual and as such have not yet been deeply understood on an emotional level.

Unconditional love is a vital part of 4D relationships. It means to love someone (and yourself) without conditions. (Note: Loving a person unconditionally does *not* mean staying when you are being abused or when you want to make a new choice.) Even if a partner does not fulfill your needs, you still love that person as an aspect of God. If the partner does not carry out your expectations, love him/her for being who he/she is without insisting on change. Unconditional love is an "in the moment" yet forever type of experience, whereas conditional love is always based upon past memories or future expectations rather than the present. Ask yourself this question: Could you love and accept your current partner unconditionally if he/she never evolved (in this life) any further from the current state of being?

Another common misperception about unconditional love has to do with personal boundaries. Loving people unconditionally does *not* mean that you allow them to victimize you. It does not mean staying with them while they continue to beat or demoralize you. Unconditional love also includes love for yourself as an equal, and you must be willing to act on maintaining your love for yourself *at the risk of the relationship*. You are an important part of the equation and not to be sacrificed.

Loving someone unconditionally can also mean leaving with love, not recriminations, when his/her actions impose themselves upon your personal boundaries. In this way you maintain your 4D quality of honesty, present a reflection for the abusers to see themselves clearly, and take action to preserve your own self-love and self-worth. Whether the partner does or does not see his/her own reflection is not your responsibility. What *is* your responsibility is honoring yourself enough to act in your best interest, which ultimately is in the best interest of all.

Martyrdom is *not* a fourth-density relationship characteristic!

Being unconditionally loving means that you love and honor yourself as much as the partner, respecting your own boundaries. Changing the form of a relationship (from lovers to friends, for instance) to honor your own needs is one possibility as long as you act out of integrity and do not shut your heart to the previous partner.

Absolute trust is the opposite of the 3D need to control. There cannot be any need or desire to control in 4D. As you work to develop honesty in your relationships, trust begins to develop naturally. If you are still engaging in dishonesty, secrecy, or conditional love, there is an inherent distrust present that keeps you anchored in 3D. This is often a difficult challenge for many. Focus not so much on learning to trust as in learning to be honest and love the self. When you do that, trust comes naturally.

Allowingness is the opposite of manipulation. Allow others to be who they need to be without trying to change them. It is only then that you will truly see who they are. If you attempt to manipulate them, you will never see who they really are, *but only who you need them to be,* which is only an illusion. This distorted perception keeps you in a loop of dishonesty with yourself and your relationship.

Relationships by Choice. This is the opposite of fear-based monogamy. This means that if you want monogamy, it is by conscious choice. If you happen to prefer polygamy or polyfidelity, it is also by conscious choice. Many people fall into relationships without evaluating what they truly want. In a sense, they take what they can get. Those types of relationships do not reinforce self-love and they perpetuate the cycle of conditional love, where one partner hopes that the other person will transform into who he or she needs them to be.

A 4D relationship requires that you clearly communicate your needs and desires for a relationship to your partner. You can no longer allow yourself to manipulate truth to get what you want. You must now make a choice and commit to it unconditionally.

It is perfectly acceptable for you to choose monogamy, polyfidelity, or any other form of relationship. All these choices are inherently neutral. They do not have a built-in meaning. You ascribe meaning to them by judgment, saying that one is "better" or "worse" than another. Any choice can work for you *as long as your choice is a conscious one.* If the choice is not conscious and you are not choosing what you desire and need, then you are being dishonest—and thus you cannot thus take full responsibility for your part in the relationship. You must then play the role of

151

victim. If your conscious choice is to move into a 4D relationship, you can no longer hold onto any 3D agendas.

You do not need to adopt these relationship characteristics immediately. This will happen naturally at your own pace. However, in the transition period now between 3D and 4D, you are being hit with challenges from both realities. As this happens, you will need to make some choices about how you wish to continue in your relationships. As you exercise your conscious choices (with love) to better yourself and your world, you will naturally begin to make choices that support the 4D-reality paradigm.

If you choose the integrative 4D model and truly become that idea (not just *try* to become it), eventually you will not feel the pain of loss in any relationship. This is where you are headed in your evolution. You feel pain or loss only when you are in a 3D relationship with all of its separative paradigms and controls or when you delude yourself into thinking you are in a 4D relationship and expecting its rewards but are disappointed because its qualities are really still 3D.

Straddling the fence can be very painful, but its gift is in providing you with a perspective into both realities at the same time. From there you can make an informed, conscious choice. Do not judge where you are now. Use your current position as a way to gain perspective into both realities so that your choices are based upon experience as well as positive and conscious evolution.

Navigating 4D Challenges

As you shift from a 3D to a 4D perspective, you will experience fear as relationships transform. You are going through uncharted territory. You cannot see what is over the next ridge and this is frightening for many people. If a 4D relationship is something you really want to pursue, then let that fear be okay. At this point, being willing to break a relationship *only* if there is another to fill that space still makes you dependent. It is taking the step *in spite of* the fear that is the key. When you come out on the other side, you will realize that your identity is not based upon another person, only you. You are the only one on which you can rely. You will feel that sense of power, clarity, and liberation that comes from recognizing your own power.

Even in 3D you create circumstances that remind you that you are all connected. For instance, people use enmeshment—unhealthy attachment—in 3D to remind themselves of that connection. However, the way you have interpreted the idea of connectedness in 3D is detrimental rather than supportive. Enmeshment is the 3D version of connectedness in 4D. The way you look at it depends on whether you see it from 3D dependency or 4D love/allowing.

When you feel enmeshed with another person in your life and it hurts, stop for a minute. Take some deep breaths. The enmeshment is there to remind you that you are ultimately never separate from the other person. Separation is an illusion. No matter how far away you go, you are not separate from the person. If you can begin to emotionally heal the fear that you will no longer be with a person in a certain way, you can begin to feel the sense of connectedness that will replace the 3D enmeshment and the fear that accompanies it. You will then feel the underlying connectedness in all of your relationships.

Relationship changes began in the 1960s, when people began to feel the shift from 3D to 4D in their emotional bodies. Since then most people have not known quite what to do with this energy. They did not understand that they could move with this energy and heal their relationships. Most tried to resist the change. The rise in divorce since the 1960s is because of the confusion that resulted from the new energy and people's subsequent attempts at conscious evolvement by breaking their bonds with the past.

Divorce, in its stereotypically unpleasant, recriminating form, is a 3D solution. Divorce is the formal act of separating oneself to artificially create the illusion that one is no longer connected to another person. The 4D version of divorce is the recognition by both parties that the relationship is progressing in a different direction and actions are being taken for such a transition.

Ultimately, there is no such thing as separation, because you can never truly be separate from anyone or anything. In 4D you will easily be able to allow others to move in a needed direction. Even when a couple no longer manifests their life as partners, they have not separated in the cosmic sense because separation is only an illusion. The couple simply chooses not to live their lives as partners in an outward manifestation, but they honor the past

153

association and remain unconditionally loving and supportive in their hearts.

Everyone has been touched by these new energies and responds to them in the only way they know how. Some people deny them. Others become polarized. Still others go with the flow. This issue will not go away. It is going to challenge you again and again until you come face to face with your own feelings of inadequacy and aloneness and acknowledge how you have sought relationships to fill that gap. You will create less disharmony if you move with it. By resisting it, you create more discomfort and pain.

Many people believe that relationship choices such as monogamy, polyfidelity, or divorce have only to do with sex, but there is a deeper meaning. Individuals frequently ascribe superficial meaning to a circumstance so that it can be used as a distraction from inner pain and so that they feel they have a handle on it. Here is an example. If a man has an affair, his wife might easily conclude that her husband just wanted sex instead of looking deeply into her own unhappiness in the relationship.

Sex, however, is an expression of vulnerability and frequently pushes people's buttons. Most people avoid vulnerability, and they certainly do not want their partners being vulnerable with other people! Sex is not the issue and never has been. Putting the blame on sex is a cover for a greater, unacknowledgeable fear. Your points of view on sex as a society are symptoms of a deeper dysfunction and have nothing to do with infidelity.

Humans experience internal changes but might first notice them as external changes. You might think it is a problem with your relationship, but it is not. You will see the subtle internal changes in yourself and your partner reflected in your relationship. The first level of change will always be inside you, but you might not be aware of it until it is triggered externally. If you resist change you will start feeling pain, confusion, and maybe even manifest all sorts of physical symptoms. This will happen if you are not willing to move with the changes occurring inside you and the mass consciousness.

If you are willing to move with change, you might become more emotional for a while. You might begin to release old issues, and at that point your relationships will begin to change. Change does not mean that relationships will end or that there will be a divorce.

Change simply means change, that is all. If there is a partner in your life, you can seek to help them move through changes at the same time you do. Trust that the two of you are on the same path no matter what happens or how the changes manifest.

Some people base personal satisfaction or success on how their relationships are progressing. For instance, if there is no conflict, then there are presumably no imbalances. This old belief system can at times delude you into remaining in a relationship that is disempowering to you. That method of gauging can no longer continue. This artificial construct gives you artificial data so you do not have to face your fears. That was a tool in 3D but in 4D it is very different. You will see that if you resist claiming your own power, you will continually seek relationships only to validate yourself. If relationships continue to fail and you have continual conflict, you are still using the relationship to make you feel better. That cannot occur in a 4D relationship because self-honesty is of utmost importance.

Commitment and Conscious Choice

Stressing the importance of conscious choice in relationships does not mean that there must be a conditional acceptance from both parties. Here is an example of conscious choice. Let's say that you are in a relationship and you say to your partner, "I want a monogamous (or polygamous) relationship, and I will continue this relationship with you only if you agree to it." You have a situation that does not work.

Choices you make can be only for yourself, otherwise you are controlling the relationship—which is a 3D idea. You cannot impose your choices on another. If you choose monogamy, then that means it is only *you* who chooses not to have sex with others. You cannot require the other person to make the same choice. The partner needs to freely make his or her own choices, otherwise he/she will not be fully present in the relationship. However, you might clearly choose not to enter into a relationship with a person who chooses a lifestyle that is not to your taste. That is quite all right. It is only about *you!* Your choices are all for *you;* they have nothing to do with the other person. People often get so caught up in controlling the choices of their partners that they lose control of their own lives, and that is where most of the problems in

155

relationships lie. In this case you can see that a truly healthy and successful relationship will come through compatible and conscious choices made by both parties.

In 4D relationships commitment as you have defined it in the past will not exist. The old definition of commitment takes you out of the present. In 3D relationships commitment was often seen as a burden imposed by the partner! When people make a healthy commitment in 4D, it will be because they want to better themselves and the relationship through 4D principles. A 3D commitment often vows, "I promise to stay with you until death." A 4D commitment might say, "I am committed to growing in this relationship and seeing it as a reflection of my relationship with the divine. I commit myself to act with integrity and respect in all of my interactions."

The old definition of commitment is a 3D illusion. It keeps you feeling safe in the moment, but does it *really* ever turn out the way you hope? How many people make commitments that do not last? A commitment never ensures your security; it simply deludes you into *thinking* you are secure. That is the difference. In 3D security does not exist, as it is defined by fear, and fear will always undermine one's feeling of security.

The only true commitments are personal covenants between the ego and the higher self. These covenants remind you how to conduct relationships in a way that ensure the continuation of your own growth, integrity, and responsibility. These commitments are made to the self instead of the other person. Commitments made to the self tap a deep inner power and strength. They never create resentment toward another human being.

Being Fully Yourself

One of the greatest gifts you can give the people in your life is by being fully *you*. This means being absolutely honest, respectful, and loving in all interactions and not taking responsibility for their pain.

To use an illustration, let us say that you are walking down the street and you see a friend. You say, "Oh, you got a haircut. It looks nice." The friend gets upset, thinking you are patronizing him. His reaction is totally unexpected. All of you have had experiences like this when you have been totally misunderstood. You might have said something with love and with no ill intent, yet somehow you pushed a button in the other person.

What are you going to do? Will you stop speaking to other people to avoid pushing one of those unseen buttons? No, you must at all costs express yourself with integrity and not take responsibility for a possible reaction. You never truly know how another person will react because that person's programming is different from yours. The challenge here is to be very, very clear. In order to accomplish honesty in a 4D way, there must be no hidden agenda or ulterior motive in your comments. People often have unconscious (or even conscious) agendas, which might include wanting to avenge a grievance, to belittle another to boost their own ego, or to control another's behavior. All humans at one time or another have engaged in these actions. If you can allow yourself to admit this, you are that much closer to clear and honest communication—and to an open humility.

The greatest service you can provide to your neighbor is by being fully who you are. Let us give you an example, using a fictional model. Let us say that a woman is afraid of heights. She came into this life to resolve a lifetime in which she jumped off a cliff. Let us also say that her husband recognizes that she is afraid of heights, so he makes sure she is never around anything high. How can she confront what she came here to face if her husband keeps steering her away from her fears? It makes it more difficult and prolongs the pain.

Perhaps one day the husband says, "I want to go hot-air ballooning. Do you want to come with me?" She might actually say yes because she recognizes it as a way to face her fear. In this case she cannot do that unless the husband gives her the opportunity to face those issues rather than protecting her from them.

This is what is meant by enmeshment—when you have lost the boundaries between yourself and others. You try to protect other people, but in reality you are really trying to protect yourself from their anger, disapproval or invalidation of you. In this case the husband thinks he is protecting his wife from her fear. What he is really doing is protecting himself from witnessing her emotional pain. He might even feel guilty, somehow thinking *he* caused her pain! He was protecting himself and at the same time enabling his wife to continue being afraid and avoid her fears—when that is what she came here to face!

The biggest gift you can give anyone in your life is to be fully who you are. You will be challenged to go beyond your perceived limitations and take responsibility for your life, your fears and emotions. Your emotions and reactions are never caused by someone outside of you. They all come from *you*. The greatest gift you can give in a relationship is to never hold back who you really are—your honest feelings and thoughts—because you feel that what you say might cause pain.

There is a big difference between deliberately causing emotional hurt to someone and being who you know yourself to be. An example of deliberately hurting someone emotionally would be if the husband dragged the wife to the top of the cliff and forced her to look over the edge. Being who he naturally is does not hurt her. If she chooses to be hurt, it is her choice to interpret circumstances in that way. Emotionally, there are no victims. People are never emotional victims when they choose to engage in a situation but do not exercise their own empowerment.

If you believe that one person can hurt another person emotionally, then you create a polarity between victims and perpetrators. In a sense, that belief is demoralizing because it assumes that humans are weak and powerless even though they are actually beings of spirit and light. The condition of victimization has been glamorized in your society to the point where empowerment has been totally misunderstood and ignored. The answer to victimization is not a lawsuit but the inherent power within each soul to make conscious and informed choices. Until the human race truly embraces self-empowerment, victimization will be glamorized and rewarded and you will move further and further away from a 4D reality.

You cannot walk on eggshells around each other any longer. You might never be able to anticipate what will hurt your mate. In your innocence and excitement you might take him/her to one of those cliffs not knowing about that fear. Can you protect yourself from such a situation? The only thing you can be is fully who you are—*that* is empowerment. This means disengaging yourself from the covert attachments you have with people and recognizing the deeper spiritual connections you have always had.

When you withhold a part of yourself, you compromise your integrity. If you do not express who you are, you are effectively lying to yourself and to the other person. They cannot ever love you for who you truly are because they do not *know* who you truly are.

Withholding your true feelings for fear of hurting another (or being rejected) is a 3D idea. You cannot carry this behavior into 4D if you want to truly express yourself. Self-empowered people would never be hurt by the well-meaning comment of another when it is said with love and not malice. This is because they recognize that *they* cocreate all comments that are made. They are the ones generating their reality. They cannot be a victim of their own creations!

When you withhold your truth, it buries itself in your cells. It begins building toxins, first on the emotional level, and then it will show up on the physical level. If you do not express who you are fully, you must store the withheld energy inside you. It can eat you alive. Cancer, heart disease and other ailments are a result of a self-judgment that you are not worthy to be fully who you know yourself to be. The more you repress it, the more diseased you become.

Releasing your true self eventually leads to ecstasy.

Expressing Your Truth

You can retrain yourself to know who you are and act on that knowledge. The first step can occur in a confrontative situation. First, think about what you want to say. (Many people do not let themselves think about what they *really* want to say. They repress it before they become fully aware of it.) Write it down. Say it into a tape recorder. Get comfortable with who you are. Learn to express yourself without the heavy self-judgments you have made in the past. If you are not allowing yourself even to think your truth, you certainly cannot train yourself to speak it. Let it be okay to be aware of your truth. Keep a journal to externalize it. By doing this, you place your truth outside of your energy field so it doesn't lodge in your energy body.

When you deny any part of yourself, you shut off the very foundation of your creative energy. You judge that only parts of you are worthy and other parts are not. This throws you into disharmony; therefore, all of your relationships will reflect the disharmony you are feeling internally. You cannot withhold any portion of your truth without damaging yourself.

Eventually you will be able to tell the difference between a balanced and integrated communication and one where you are attacking or manipulating. The more you practice, the more you will be able to discern. If you want to take gradual steps toward expressing who you are, then center yourself before you speak. From that place of centeredness ask yourself if what you have to say is balanced and integrated, or if you have a desire to control the other person through your expression.

If your desire to communicate is connected to wanting the other person to change who they are, then it is a manipulative communication. If you can see that your desire for communication is not clean, at least own or acknowledge this by expressing it to yourself. Listen to your thoughts and feelings. Your relationships will blossom and change when you learn to communicate in clean and clear ways. This means that you must begin to understand and take responsibility for your hidden agendas and unspoken desires.

Before you express something, ask yourself what your goal is. Sometimes you might find that you want to change the other person. Sometimes you can see it, other times you cannot. When you cannot see your hidden agendas but express your thoughts anyway, then do not worry about making a "wrong" move. If you honestly cannot see it, then you are not deliberately hurting the other person, though you are still responsible for the communication. If the expression is an attack, you have offered the other person a way to heal their beliefs about being attacked by providing the stimulus. Through that person's reaction you will learn how to communicate with clarity and without manipulation.

Whether it is an attack or a clean expression, you provide a way for the other person to learn and to grow. If they have no issue about being attacked, they are not going to feel attacked. If they believe they *can* be attacked and that is one of their issues, they will feel attacked. You cannot take responsibility for how the person reacts, only for how cleanly you communicate. Your interactions with each other are choreographed in perfect synchronicity according to what lessons need to be learned.

Even though it is not possible to know all the time what will hurt another person, one thing that will always hurt you is dishonesty with yourself and those you care about. You might walk up to your spouse (who is feeling absolutely joyous and ecstatic) and say, "You look like a pig today." If a person feels really good about him or herself, that comment will not hurt in the least. You cannot ever know what will hurt another person, so stop trying to take responsibility for their reactions! It is far more beneficial to take responsibility for yourselves and *your* reality.

This in and of itself can be a great freedom, because it is a way to reclaim your power. Recognize that the primary intention here is never to destroy but always to love. Even the most heinous acts are to learn love. That is the most fundamental intention of creation. Every action is based upon the intention of learning to love. Examine your beliefs. If you really know that God is an expression of love, then every action must ultimately support that belief. If you believe instead that words or actions can hurt others and there is no higher purpose, then there must be a belief somewhere inside you that says God can be uncaring or hurtful.

No other person truly knows what will hurt you. To withhold a comment because it might hurt someone is assuming responsibility for their emotions and thus their growth. No human need accept responsibility for another person's growth. To do so would actively inhibit and sabotage that person's growth and the things he/she has chosen to confront.

As people move from third to fourth density, you might feel hurtful emotions. It is almost the same as when you get frostbite. Once you warm up, you get the feeling back in your feet and they really begin to hurt. It is a significator. Some are using the hurt that way—to remind themselves that they can still feel.

When you totally embrace fourth-density relationships, you will not feel the same pain you did with third-density concepts. Some people hold onto portions of third density as they are grasping for fourth density, so they feel much pain—this is an indicator of the change. However, if you are still experiencing pain, struggle, or deception, go back and examine your premises and actions. You will likely find that you have still been operating from a 3D-reality paradigm.

161

You will see changes when you begin to recognize the times when you are operating from third-density principles and are attempting to bring them into a fourth-density relationship. As you begin changing because of those realizations, you will see tremendous and powerful changes in your life. Do not be surprised. Those changes will bring ecstasy and joy. Growth does not have to bring pain.

The twenty-year period from 1992 to 2012 is critical. There will be more stress in relationships that resist change. Actual societal change regarding relationships will come about by necessity. This can take the form of family restructuring because of single parents, working parents, or financial concerns. However, what brings about real changes in relationships will not be these external things but the internal momentum of the change in your energy. The external things are only symptoms of that change.

The transformation to fourth density is going to happen. It will happen more quickly as people consciously make choices to pursue fourth-density ideas. It will take longer if they resist the flow. A critical mass is going to be reached that will set the tide in motion on a mass scale. It is just a question of when. This depends upon whether you choose to take the bull by the horns or run away from the bull. Either way, evolution cannot be denied.

Fulfilling Your Needs

Humans often judge the idea of *need* in relationships to be negative, but it does not have to be. Fourth density means integration. Third density means separation. Separation is like all the soup ingredients sitting separately on a counter; integration is like the soup. As you move from 3D to 4D and seek to become whole, you must first recognize what the recipe requires. The recipe needs carrots and celery. If you recognize those needs, you will chop them up and throw them into the pot. The soup will then become the true expression of who you are in an integrated way.

If you do not want to acknowledge your needs, you will not know the recipe, you will not know how to cook the soup, and it will take a lot more energy, pain and struggle to eventually try to guess the recipe. The fulfillment of healthy needs is important for the eventual goal of integration. You might not appreciate your needs right now, but they are a valuable part of the entire experience of who you are in the long run.

Your needs in and of themselves are neutral. They are an extension of your emotional health. They have no value except what you ascribe to them. You cannot judge those carrots on the counter as being wrong. Your needs are like those carrots. They are ideas that will be put into a pot and eventually become a valuable creation. Nothing exists without a purpose, and your needs are still part of that soup.

It is very important that you read those lines in the recipe (i.e., your needs), chop up the vegetables, and make them a part of the soup you are attempting to create. Once your needs are validated and put into the pot, the cooking process transforms them into something wonderful. If they are not allowed in the pot, they will never transform.

What wonderful experiences await you! Third-density relationships can be painful. There is an old saying, "If you cannot feel the pain, you cannot feel the ecstasy." In fourth density that idea does not exist. You have a tremendous amount of love and joy locked within you that will begin to blossom when you stop expecting another person to validate you and make you feel whole. As that idea is relinquished, you will soar.

As you move into 4D you will contain so much love that it is beyond what you can now conceive. You are moving in that direction, and those who choose to embrace the fourth-density idea (by diving right in or by taking baby steps) will begin seeing immediate changes.

You will feel these changes internally. The pain will start to subside and the joy will begin to grow. As this happens you will begin to see your divine connection reflected in the eyes of those you love.

163

13

NAVIGATING
THE PATH OF LIFE

Those who have studied metaphysics understand that there is
no such thing as a random event. You are the cocreator of your
universe and all events are created so you can learn from them in
one way or another.

Some events are *seemingly* random. For instance, you might be
cooking dinner and spill a cup of water. This "accident" might not
have an immediate significance and you might be unable to see
any connection whatsoever with your reality. You call these *random events*. These experiences can affect you in a positive, negative or neutral way.

The Meaning of Random Events

As the mass consciousness is growing and transforming, the
definition of these types of events will change. Let us begin by
examining *random negative events*.

From the time you were born, society has taught you to withhold
your emotions. As you go through life, some emotions are expressed and others repressed. This is not even a conscious decision. Because of these repressed emotions, there is a wellspring
within you that needs to be periodically released. This can be done
in various ways, and one way is through sickness or disease.

Events that seem trivial might have a greater significance when
viewed from a different perspective. These random events (like
dropping something on your toe) trigger an emotion. The emotion
might be anger, fear, or helplessness. The emotions triggered by

random events are part of the process of releasing stored energy suppressed in the human body and energy field. It is essential that you allow yourself to feel these spontaneous surges of emotion, then move on. These releases help you stay balanced both emotionally and energetically in the challenging world of physical life on Earth.

Some people create a tremendous number of random negative events—events that might not seem related but are experienced all at once. When this happens it is as if there is a message from the unconscious world attempting to make itself known. Those individuals who repeatedly manifest random negative events most likely have so much repressed emotion (because they do little personal processing) that these releases become necessary to maintain a healthy and stable emotional environment. In this case random negative events are of tremendous value. Until these people can heed the messages of their higher consciousness, random negative events will continue as a way to teach lessons of the self and ensure that their emotional energy does not become blocked.

Humans are working toward the integration of their mental, emotional, spiritual and physical selves. Simultaneous to your move from third to fourth density, there is a sense of letting go of the old way of being. Part of your letting go means that you must understand that things occur in your reality for specific learning. When you understand your experiences on a deeper level, you allow the experiences to affect your evolution. Random events will become less relevant to 3D reality as you all become more of your full self.

Random events occur much less often in fourth density. As you become more aware of your soul and your integrative process in 4D, they will not be necessary as learning tools. It is only in a reality where you are still questioning your own power as a creator that you need such manifestations.

On the other side of the coin, there are also *random positive events.* For instance, someone might give you a bright and brilliant smile on the street as you walk by. There might be a deeper meaning there for you. If you cannot find a deeper meaning, it might simply be one of those random events created by your soul to release an emotion. Perhaps on that day it was necessary for you to feel a sense of joy or a sense of being loved by other people. Your soul will create this type of incident for a needed emotional experience.

Human emotions are a way to bring your soul's energy into physicality. This is why the expression of emotion is so important in human development starting at birth. The more you allow emotion to pass through you, the greater control and mastery you will feel. You will be master of your emotions rather than their servant. Emotions master you only when you do not allow them to express themselves naturally in the moment.

When something unexpected happens that seems to have come out of nowhere, understand that whether it is positive, negative, or neutral, it has a vital role in your life and your expression as a soul. There is no need to understand these events intellectually. It is more important that you express whatever emotional energy surges through you at the time.

There are two types of random creation—informational and experiential. In informational creations, knowledge comes to you in symbolic form, such as through the rolling of dice or the reading of tarot cards. It is usually a communication, random, but direct. It is up to you to learn your inner language of symbology to interpret the message clearly.

Experiential creations include those seemingly random events whose purpose is to allow you to experience emotion without having to understand why. Examples might include dropping something on your toe or breaking an object. Even receiving a beautiful smile from a stranger might fall into this category, though the person is possibly someone you know on a soul level. The anger expressed or felt when you stubbed your toe was exactly what you needed to clear your emotional body. Emotion is a biochemical reaction; you create pain to create an emotional/biochemical response.

Another reason for stubbing your toe might be that your soul is trying to communicate with you. (This would be an informational creation.) For instance, let's say you stub your right toe. Because people usually lead with their right foot, this might be an indication that you have a fear of stepping forward or that you are trying to go forward too fast and it is not the correct timing. It depends on the circumstance. Ultimately, you never have to mentally understand the message clearly as long as you feel its impact.

In your nonphysical state of existence there is no sense of randomness, because you become totally aware of yourself as the creator of reality down to the very last detail. In your nonphysical state there would be no reason for the jar of water to fall from the counter if you did not deliberately create it to do so. This is one of the main reasons why you as a lightbeing have chosen a reality of limitation and semiamnesia. It gives you a new way to learn about yourselves through the discovery that you do indeed create your reality—a fact that you know but have temporarily forgotten! This is the lure of physical reality—to test the self and your ability amidst chaos to remember your origins.

Do not be too hard on yourself if you do not always understand the message behind an incident. Let us say that you spill some water, but there is no emotional charge. In that case it would be more of a symbolic communication connected with water. As you clean up the water, you might be thinking about twelve other things, but your soul is communicating with you by at least partially focusing your attention on the water.

Ultimately, it is never necessary to understand the symbology intellectually as long as you are present in the moment with the symbol rather than focusing on the past or the future. Taking yourself out of the moment includes judging yourself for spilling the water or blaming someone else for putting it on the counter.

There are times when it would greatly help you to understand the message. At these times you will receive the messages clearly as long as you are open and receptive. You cannot ever really miss anything! It is all a matter of trusting that you get what you need when you need it—whether it is obvious symbology for the mind to chew on or subtle symbology to be absorbed by your subconscious.

Humans can become obsessed with figuring out every symbol in their lives. They might spend more time thinking about the symbol that happened yesterday (taking themselves out of the moment) than attending to what is happening in their reality now. You always get what you need when you need it. You are always receiving communication from your higher aspects. There is never a moment that you are not. If you do not get it the first time, it will come again and again.

It might be of interest to study how another culture (such as the Pleiadians) process what you consider negative emotion. Though they can experience anger (and sometimes do) their sense of emotionality is more homogeneous than yours. You label each emotion, but to them, the edges of those labels blend, so there is no sense of pure anger in a separate form as you have here. The easiest way to describe their experience would be as a combination of anger and ecstasy. The best explanation is that there is anger at the time the event happens (like spilling the water) and joy that tension is released.

For the Pleiadians, the emotion passes quickly. Their definitions of emotions are more malleable than yours. But you are changing, and once you purge what has been suppressed, your emotional body will become more malleable as well. You will be able to express emotions very differently.

Understanding the Obstacles of Life

You all cocreate life's events together. Imagine that you drop a stone into a pool, causing ripples. *You* are the stone that causes the ripples in the pool. The shape of the ripples and the intensity of the wave force are *your* creation. Therefore, *your* universe is arranged according to *your* creation. However, other people are causing their own ripples as well. The realm in which you meet is the cocreative reality.

You can also view this in terms of you and your higher self. There is a realm known as the cocreative realm. Let us say your soul (or higher self) built the hallway you will travel in any given lifetime. No matter what happens, you *will* go down that hallway. However, you as the personality or ego can choose to move down the hallway any way you wish. You can run, walk, do cartwheels, swim, crawl. You can do it easily or you can struggle. That is the nature of your freedom of choice.

You create obstacles though your free will. However, you can also navigate your life's path without them. So what is the secret? In order to smoothly transition into fourth density and begin truly feeling your powers as a creator, it requires one thing: You must be fully willing to look at your shadow.

You must be so committed to your own growth that you are willing to risk everything you have created to keep the illusion of safety intact—whether it be relationships, the mask of your self-created persona, or your meticulously created defense mechanisms. You must be willing to see yourself without illusion. At first the vision of the self might be hideous, because you are so used to protecting yourself from your own pain. However, as you begin to work with it and love it through its healing process, the reflection of yourself will be more beautiful than you can possibly imagine.

You can avoid looking at yourself truthfully for only a limited time, even though it might span lifetimes. For many people these personal challenges are like walking down a hallway and seeing a big rock in the way. Because that rock is covered with slimy moss, you might fear that it is difficult to climb.

Here is the challenge. If you look at that rock and say, "I can't do it; it's too slimy. I don't want to get my clothes dirty," then your perception of the challenge will make you feel limited. If you perceive the challenge as being something that will give you a gift (and you can anticipate the wonderful things that await you beyond it), then your positive perception of the challenge will keep your vision unlimited. It's not so much that the challenges are illusions, but that the energy you attach to them is an illusion. The challenge itself is neutral, but you can attach a perception of limitation to it that makes it *feel* like a negative challenge.

Many people are hard on themselves when they encounter a rock in the hallway, as if that somehow means they have failed as a spiritual being. True spiritual beings embrace the rock because it allows them to better themselves! When the rock is embraced and perceived as a tool that will provide immense growth (and therefore joy), there is no pain associated with it.

If the rock is there, it needs to exist. Many times you forget that you have entered this life in partnership with your soul. Between you there is a sense of trust and love. Your ego personality says, "But I don't remember choosing this." You can get stuck on that protest and resistance if you wish, but it will not serve you in the long run.

170

What *will* serve you is taking those challenges and perceiving them in a way that allows you to feel limitless. The more limitless you feel, the more your hallway expands, and the rocks you have put in your path will diminish in size. But when your perception keeps you limited, each rock becomes a mountain.

Surrendering to the flow of life allows you unlimited thought. Surrendering does not mean letting go of everything and hiding in your closet, waiting for reality to come to you. Surrendering also does not mean waiting for someone to save you. Surrendering means letting go of the resistance to the natural flow of your life. If you use the natural current as the source of energy that takes you down the river of life (while still taking responsibility to steer the boat), then you have created a beautiful marriage between spirit and human action.

Surrendering is only one part of the equation. Intention and action are equal elements, without which you are not grounded in physical reality. In using the hallway analogy, intention is expressed by looking down that hallway and saying, "Yes, the current is carrying me down this hallway. I surrender to the current, but I will steer." *That* is an expression of intention.

If you forget your intention, you will bump around, not realizing you can take action and get yourself on the best, most balanced course for you. Intention and action are an essential part of surrender, because without them the spirit and the human realities cannot be integrated. This is an example of how what sounds like a paradox is actually a key to transformation.

The Concept of Karma

There has been much misunderstanding surrounding the concept of karma. Some people have viewed it as a form of cosmic punishment whereas others have seen it as an archaic Eastern belief that has no place in the modern Western world. The analogy of "an eye for an eye" is often used to illustrate the principle. For those people who still need to believe in a punishing and authoritative God, that two-dimensional definition has provided security.

At higher levels of understanding each person is responsible for his own actions. Between lives each soul chooses its earthly challenges in order to learn the lessons it feels it needs. No one

punishes another, although some souls choose to punish themselves. To embrace the higher teachings of karma, one must
surrender all notions of not being responsible for one's own creations.

Karma is not about being a victim of cause and effect. To use an
analogy, stretch a rubber band between your hands. The physical
law of cause and effect says that when you let go of the rubber
band it will snap back at you. If you stretch the rubber band taut
and keep holding it, relaxing slowly, then you have consciously
made a decision through wisdom, because you chose an outcome
that would create balance. Wisdom erases karma, so to speak.
Patterns that have been laid out before your birth need not be
mindlessly followed as if you are a puppet of the universe.

When awareness is expressed through love, it becomes wisdom.
Wisdom balances karma.

When awareness is expressed, there does not need to be a
mindless cause-and-effect reaction. This is how you become a
conscious director of the flow of your life. You have the option of
using your awareness, expressing it through love and achieving
wisdom. This balances karma, and you no longer need to be the
victim of mindless cause-and-effect lessons throughout time. Thus
as lessons are learned, you are able to make present choices from
a position of integrity and responsibility. You no longer incur
karma that will have to be balanced later. Instead, all of your
actions become heart-centered and carry you quickly to the next
step of your evolution.

Following Your Excitement

Fourth-density reality is based on the idea of following your
excitement with responsibility. This leads to a natural flow of
activity and growth lessons. As you become more and more adept
at living in fourth density, you will find that synchronicity works
hand in hand with your own natural excitement. This of course
requires a lot of trust. You do not need to master this right away.
In fact, the true understanding of this model and all of its implications can take many years to grasp.

Let us present a model that will eventually replace the current
lifestyle on Earth. This new lifestyle allows for deep growth

lessons, but with it comes total and unconditional self-responsibility. There can never be any blame or victimhood because there are only sovereign beings. This is part of the package deal in fourth density. Pain is caused when people do not follow their excitement because they do not acknowledge what gives them joy and happiness. Give yourself permission to begin this process, even in the smallest of ways. Your awareness will blossom and lead you further and further into a sense of your own empowerment.

Imagine that when you are in your excitement the life force is flowing fully through you. You are empowered as a divine being. When you are *not* following your excitement, you are getting merely a tiny stream of energy from your divine self. This energy is just enough to animate you and keep you here on Earth. Under those circumstances it is very difficult to go forward with the goals you have brought with you into this life.

Learn to follow your excitement in the moment (with responsibility) in every aspect of your life. Your reality will shift and change as you do. This might seem impractical in relation to the constraints of your life at work on a day-to-day basis, so begin by practicing in small increments. Here is an exercise that will assist you.

FOLLOWING YOUR EXCITEMENT
(Exercise)

Take a whole day for this exercise. This day will be totally devoted to following your excitement. This means that the minute you open your eyes in the morning you will say to yourself, "What do I feel like doing? Well, I feel like reading this book." Pick up the book and begin reading.

Here is the catch: Many of you say to yourself mentally, "After I finish this chapter, I'm going to go into the kitchen and get some juice." That statement is *not* an expression of following your excitement in the moment. When you feel the desire for juice, simply put the book down and go get the juice. Drink your juice until you feel the excitement to go turn on the television or wherever your excitement takes you next. Do not in any way plan ahead.

Examine your feelings during this daylong exercise. You might find emotions of guilt, confusion, or panic begin to emerge. If so, do not be concerned. These emotions are not signs of failure with the exercise, but of success! In today's busy world humans have moved so far away from hearing the voice of their soul (which often uses excitement as a communication tool) that when they begin to align with the soul once again, a sense of panic overshadows the experience. By practicing this exercise, you will be able to reconnect with the joyful voice of the soul once again.

Practice this exercise for an entire day. Try to stay in the moment as much as possible. The goal does not lie in any particular outcome, but in the experience itself.

       ✿   ✿   ✿

To help clarify this exercise, let us say that you want to go to the sea. Use this excursion to practice this exercise. Get yourself ready, pack your picnic basket, and go down to the train station. A train might not be leaving for an hour, but do not be attached to when you should leave or how bored you will be while you wait. Stay in the present. *Follow the excitement of what is available to you at any given moment.*

Because the train is not leaving for an hour, it must mean there is something else to do now. So what excites you? Perhaps you would like to read the book you brought with you. When your excitement diminishes, there will be another event to draw your attention and excitement. Perhaps the train will arrive or you will become intrigued with watching the other passengers. When you decide to go to the seashore, do not attach yourself to the outcome of arriving, because that attachment leads you out of the present moment. The decision to go to the seashore is simply the direction you choose to travel in your life on that particular day. The importance does not lie in your arrival but in the experiences along the way.

The idea of following your excitement with responsibility needs to be defined here. True soul excitement will never entail coercion or forcing your intentions upon another human being. Also, being a responsible 4D individual means that all commitments and responsibilities continue to be honored.

In practicing this concept, it is tempting to use the idea of following one's excitement as a justification for irresponsible action. This is why this concept is difficult and only works well for individuals who are self-responsible and have mastered their ego games. Fourth density is not a realm of irresponsible freedom. In actuality, a fourth-density existence means that you become more responsible than ever—for your actions, intentions, and the influence you have over others. Fourth density means that as a species, humans must now enter adulthood by walking their talk and taking responsibility.

If all members of society were free to do what excites them, would anything ever get done? When allowed to come into balance naturally, nothing will remain in an unbalanced state. Circumstances appear out of balance only when an unnatural condition is forced upon them. Because everyone is part of the holistic planetary system, all your excitements are entwined together into a balanced whole. You will find that everything gets done. Synchronicity would be constant if you allowed it. The only difference is that you would be *happier!*

A spark of the Creator is inside you. It gives you the strength to stand as free, sovereign beings and move forward with joy and ecstasy. The changes yet to come will not overpower you. You have created these challenges for your own growth and learning, and you are fully capable and empowered to confront them and become the beautiful beings you truly are—beings of light and love who are connected to all of creation.

14

BECOMING WHOLE

Humans incarnate into this physical reality so that the soul can learn from the experience. However, the way the soul learns differs from how the ego perceives and learns from physical reality. The soul and the ego necessarily perceive existence differently.

Souls have a bird's-eye view. They can see that if you take the road on the left, it will lead to a specific place. If you take the road on the right, it leads to a different place. Thought it has this broader perspective, the soul cannot experience the same intensity of emotion you do on the physical plane.

In physicality, emotion is much more polarized. Each emotion exists within its own encapsulated idea. When you are happy, you are not sad. When you are feeling true love, you are not in fear. You cannot experience both polarities of one emotion at the same time. You usually bounce back and forth between polarities. From the soul's realm, emotions are more fluid and malleable; they can exist and be expressed simultaneously, because the soul does not exist within linear time. Even though your soul experiences pain in a less polarized way than you do, it does experience it.

There is a natural communication between the soul and its physical counterpart. When you have a physical experience, it is communicated to the soul via an archetypal language used by the unconscious. When the soul receives this translation of the human experience, it evaluates the experience through its perceptions and wisdom. It balances the energy in a way that the personality might not yet have learned how to do.

After this energy is balanced on the soul level, it is sent back to you. After you have gone through intense emotional situations, some of you have felt a sense of peace, silence, or emptiness. You feel this stillness when you receive communication from the soul. It is very subtle. It usually takes the form of pure energy rather than an emotional, symbolic, or mental form.

During such a time, sit with the stillness and let it wash over you. Open yourself to receive whatever gifts the universe wishes to send. If you can allow yourself a certain amount of detachment, you will see a stream of emotions wash over you instead of through you. You will gain the ability to watch them as if they are a movie on a screen. These emotions might be yours, but you will no longer be anchored to them. It is at this point that you see reality through the eyes of the soul.

View your soul as a partner who helps you synthesize your emotional experiences on Earth. Your soul takes these experiences (which might seem very polarized or painful), synthesizes them into a fluid and more balanced energy, then feeds this energy back to you.

Once you receive this energy, it is up to you to choose whether you wish to recycle it back into a frenzy of polarized emotions. If you do, then the cycle continues. But you can choose instead to use the period of stillness described above as a way to integrate the emotion by perceiving it from a state of detachment, acknowledging it, learning from it, and moving forward. In this way you will learn a new and direct way to communicate with your soul. Meditation has been valuable for some people because it allows the above process to occur. It is not the only way. But any type of self-reflection assists this process.

The Evolution of Emotional Cycles

For example, let us say that you experience a car accident, a very emotional experience. Your ego would feel a lot of polarized emotion such as anger, frustration, helplessness and so on. *It is important that you express this emotion.* All of these feelings are fed to the soul to be processed.

The soul cannot comprehend intense, polarized human emotion. It must translate it into a language it understands—the language of metaphor, symbolism and archetypes. Once the soul has translated an emotion into its own language, it then learns from the

178

experience and begins communicating back to you concepts and wisdom that can assist your healing process. This communication returns to you in the universal language of metaphor, often using archetypes. Everyone is fluent in this language, though most people have forgotten how to use it.

When your soul downloads this communication, you feel a natural stillness. During this time you are given an opportunity to see the situation through the soul's eyes. This is a tremendous point of power, where you can change your situation by changing your emotions and perceptions. If you do this, the situation shifts. If you instead choose to endlessly replay the polarized emotions, you get caught in a repeating pattern. You have probably seen some friends get caught in one of these repeating patterns of emotion from which they never seem able to break free.

To break this cycle and communicate directly with your soul, you must wait for that point of stillness. Bask in it. Hook into the frequency of the soul by watching yourself and your situation from a detached perspective. If you stay within this integrated sea of emotion (the soul's perspective), then your emotional challenges are more easily experienced. The lessons of life become less painful because you learn faster and act on what you have learned.

It is important to express your emotion *in the moment* of that experience. Some people release an emotion (such as anger) intensely, but then interfere with the natural cycle of healing. The anger is absorbed by the soul for processing and the stillness occurs, but they do not complete the cycle because they do one of the following two things.

Anchor the Emotion. These individuals ignore the stillness and force themselves to stay in the anger when they want to prove they are right, that they are a victim. (Needing to be right causes people to anchor themselves to an emotion.) This stops the healing process so the person never moves to the next level of emotional expression. This action actually creates more repressed emotion because the cycle is never completed. In this case people who have heard, "Don't repress your emotions" have mistaken it to mean "continually express your emotion" instead of "express your emotion and let it go, thus evolving forward."

Recycle the Emotion. These individuals wait until the anger cycle returns and then they recycle it. Instead of using the stillness to get to a higher level of that anger, they simply recycle it into round two because it is the only thing they know how to do. You might see this in people who continually create the same emotional cycles and do not know how to break free.

The two circumstances described above are connected and describe a situation in which the person chooses not to evolve but may not fully understand that that is the choice being made. Evolution must be experienced by choice; it does not occur by accident. If you find yourself stuck in these endless emotional loops, acknowledge that it is because *you have not yet chosen to evolve beyond them.* There is nothing wrong with this choice, for it is equal to any other and valuable for the learning it provides. When you finally tire of the game, you will make the choice. All evolution is yours and yours alone to choose.

As a physical being, you came into this world carrying the illusion of fragmentation so you could relearn integrity and journey back to wholeness. Without emotional processing as described above, aspects of the self remain separate from the whole and personality fragmentation continues. Achieving integrity is a process in which all parts of an entity join to hold itself together. Each aspect of the whole links with other parts of itself to create a matrix in which no one part is more dominant than another.

In current human personality constructs, the ego is a dominant aspect. As long as the ego dictates reality, the human experience will remain limited. The process of integration is one that requires the use of all aspects of self—the hidden and the obvious as well as the dark and light—to bind the whole being together into a healthy organism.

The *negative ego* is an aspect of the personality that has gone out of control. It limits your perceptual abilities to the physical. It also creates elaborate games to protect itself from your evolution as a complete being because it fears its own annihilation. This ego has caused chaos and confusion in the lives of many who need healing. However, before healing can be achieved, the greater self (even the positive ego) must learn to recognize the games and manipulations of the negative ego and be willing to make some important personality changes. The most important game of the negative ego is that of the facades you have built.

180

Facades and the True Self

Imagine an onion that has two main layers. First, there is an inner core that represents your true self. Then there is an outer layer that represents a facade—an illusion erected by the ego to present a specific image to the outside world. Many people create these throughout their lives to keep them from seeing their true being. A facade is the fake front of a house, as on a movie set. When you walk around to the other side, you see it is only six inches thick. It presents a convincing view from one angle, but there is truly no substance there. It is a useful exercise to ask yourself where you are building facades in your own personality.

You are brought up in a world in which it is easier to act from a facade than from the real self. Society dictates this, and people have accepted its usefulness to some degree. During your life, energy in the form of challenge bombards the outer layer of that facade. You spend a lot of time and energy keeping it intact. Bombarded by energy, the facade begins disintegrating, keeping you busy continually rebuilding its structure.

As your reality continues to shift and accelerate, the energy bombarding your facade will also begin accelerating. It will require more energy than ever before to keep it intact. If you have a lot of energy invested in a very rigid facade, all of your resources will be tapped to keep it in place.

If you instead allow yourself to move with the natural energy of this transformation from third to fourth density, the accelerated energy will help you tear down the facade to reveal the true self. This might be a very frightening idea to many of you because you have learned to fear your true selves and have given power to the facade. However, this is a necessary part of the healing process of your awakening to your full potential.

It will serve you to begin identifying where your facades lie. Where have you put a lot of energy? Is it in presenting a "nice" personality or a "spiritually enlightened" being? You must begin to differentiate between your true self—darkness and all—and the facades you have built to keep you from seeing the parts of yourself you dislike or fear. This is difficult, but it can be done. And it will require a tremendous amount of honesty.

Spontaneity and excitement are signposts to the true self; analytical self-judgment is a road map to the facade. Perhaps in the past you have had a spontaneous idea for your business, for example. For ten minutes it consumed you with excitement. Then suddenly that little voice began telling you, "You can't do that, you will lose money," or "You have no talent to see it through." The facade is built by the ego to cover its insecurities. It is not based in reality at all. If you can begin to recognize your true excitement and passion in life, you will be that much closer to touching the core of the onion—your true self.

This does not mean that every spontaneous idea or passion is meant to be acted upon. As you get more in touch with your true self, it will become clear which ones need action and which ones are meant to be enjoyed in the moment. Trust this. Do not be afraid to simply *feel* your excitement and passion without having to think you need to do anything about them. This is a powerful tool to help you disintegrate the facades.

Use this philosophy to help you understand your life and your choices. Within your personal relationships, ask yourself the following: "Am I in this relationship right now because I am excited to be in it? Does it still nurture me?" If the answer is yes, then you are tapped into the true self. If the answer is a definite no, then you might wish to seriously reconsider why you are deliberately sabotaging yourself for the sake of upholding a facade. This is not to say that you have to end the relationship when you make this discovery. However, you will need to do some soul-searching to find out if you wish to change it, grow within it, end it, or let it remain as is.

Money is a product of the facade, but true abundance is a product of the true self. Abundance is always yours as a being within creation. Money is a facade you create to show yourself a pretty picture of your abundance so you will feel secure. Money is a two-dimensional prop that either validates or deceives you into believing or doubting your ability to create abundance.

The simplest technique for working with your facades is to sit down with a notebook and begin writing. Here is a suggested exercise to assist you:

182

UNCOVERING THE FACADES
(Written Exercise)

Write down every self-image. Bare your soul. If you keep a journal, reread the entries you made when you were ill. See if you can understand what was going on in your life during that time. You will find that it most likely was a time during which you were feeding a lot of energy into your facades. Some self-images you are proud of, but those are equally limiting, though you might not think so.

Here is a list of some common facades held by even the healthiest of individuals. Use this as a guide to uncover your own.

• Nothing bothers me.

• My relationship is wonderful!

• I am very prosperous.

• I am spiritually evolved.

Write as many as you can. Trust that you know your true self better than anyone else ever could. If your desire to change and grow is sincere and stronger than your fear of change then you will be able to create powerful shifts within you that will be of tremendous help in your own healing.

☼   ☼   ☼

The irony is that these facades often represent people's highest aspirations. Ultimately, you create these facades to reflect your own potential. The ego, however, appropriates them and uses them to keep you weak. By understanding the games of the ego and tapping your own inner power, these self-images can transform from two-dimensional structures into strong foundations upon which you can base your evolution. To do this, a simple state of being is required—*faith.*

Hope and Faith

If you take a leap of faith into an idea that excites you, the momentum of the mass consciousness—as well as that of your own soul—will support you. A leap of faith does not mean a leap of hope. *A leap of hope* is when you jump into the pool with your eyes closed, saying, "I hope there is water in the pool." Faith and hope are two entirely different ideas. A leap of hope is a leap of separation. It is the kind of leap you take when you do not truly believe in yourself.

A leap of faith is the leap you make when you know that your excitement will take you where you need to go and that whatever the outcome, it is part of your path and will be fuel for your growth. In this way you take responsibility for all of your actions and for what you will learn from your choices.

For instance, perhaps you are feeling the need to take a leap of some kind, but you fear you do not yet have enough faith in yourself to execute the desired landing. Instead of simply perpetuating continual leaps of hope, take some time to work on the core issues that prevent a leap of faith. In gathering the inner tools necessary to believe in the self and release your fear, you automatically make possible a successful leap of faith.

All actions taken as a true leap of faith will manifest a desired goal. The landings will be executed perfectly. But actions taken from a leap of hope can cause difficulty and frustration. Each of you now has the responsibility to learn to love yourself and clear obstacles your own deservability and self-worth. If this is not accomplished, your manifestations will be slower and/or more difficult to achieve. People have different ways of working on themselves, and ultimately you must be your own teacher. However, here are a few suggestions.

Discern the belief systems your society has taken for granted. Many adults today carry within them ingrained beliefs that sabotage their attempts to attain self-mastery. These beliefs (carried from parents and their parents before them) might include the following:

- Success means that you must struggle and suffer.

- Wealth and happiness come at a high price.

- You deserve only a certain amount of happiness.

- Love hurts.

These are examples of old programming put into the internal computer called the subconscious mind. These beliefs or programs can run your life and keep you from experiencing personal happiness because they limit you without your knowledge. Learn to discover your unconscious internal programming. When you do, you can truly change it. You will naturally move from taking leaps of hope to leaps of faith.

Another irony is that you never truly fail. It is only the ego that perceives failure or success. From the soul's point of view, every creation you manifest is successful, because any situation needed for a lesson *always* manifests. So ultimately, whether you take a leap of faith or a leap of hope, the outcome will be the same—true self-knowledge and growth. The only difference is whether you experience joy or pain during the learning process.

You will always receive what you give. If you act through faith, your creations reflect your belief in yourself. If you act through hope, your creations reflect the doubt inherent in your hope.

Faith is not an emotion you can force yourself to feel. It emerges after you come to terms with the concept of hope and look into the mirror of your soul. Faith is a byproduct of self-knowledge. You must therefore walk the path of self-knowledge before you can truly act in faith. There are no shortcuts.

It is important to understand also that having faith does not mean relinquishing your power to someone or something else—such as by saying, "God will handle it for me." Many people confuse the idea of divine will with that of personal will. From an ego-dominated perspective, they are two entirely different things. The ego is threatened by the concept of divine will because it anticipates a loss of power. However, from the perspective of an integrated being, your personal will and divine will become one and the same. They cannot be separated. Once the ego is no longer the driving force of your reality, you will witness your divinity through your choices and actions—hence, divine will and personal will become one and the same.

15

SPIRITUAL SOVEREIGNTY

Spiritual sovereignty is an empowered state resulting from the wisdom gained as one truly understands one's connection to the universe. This leads to a sense of freedom brought about through a process of emotional clearing. Full spiritual sovereignty occurs when one evolves beyond the ego's need to blame and manipulate and when a deep revelation occurs in which the self fully understands its role as the sole creator of its reality. In this state the realization of self-responsibility and self-determination cannot be denied. The full impact of being responsible for one's actions and choices is finally recognized.

For the purposes of the following discussion, some definitions will be presented. They are given as tools to illustrate the principles of spiritual sovereignty.

Privilege: A privilege represents formal permission granted by an authority so a person can enjoy a status set apart for those so permitted, or so one can perform an act that would otherwise be considered "illegal" by the authority. Often when gaining a privilege, one must give up a natural right. For example, all of mankind has the natural right to join in love with another. However, under the law created by man, one must gain formal permission—a privilege—by obtaining a marriage license from a "duly constituted authority."

Right: A right is an expression of a natural state of being, recognized or unrecognized, that all humans inherently possess. For example, the right to fall in love is obvious, but not necessarily recognized by authorities. Rights can also be an extension of universal law. Rights are nullified when they are exchanged for privileges because an authoritarian, man-made body then regulates it. (An example would be when one enters into a contract with the state through a marriage license.) When natural rights are exchanged for man-made privileges granted from an outside source, humans become nonsovereign—subjects of the authority that has given the privilege. Thus they are no longer responsible for themselves.

Civil Law: Civil law is a man-made structure that organizes, controls, punishes, and rewards individuals who have given up their rights in exchange for privileges. It ensures that humans remain dependent upon an authority rather than encourages self-responsibility.

Common Law: The spirit of common law is based upon the idea of self-responsibility and natural rights. It is recognized under the United States Constitution as being the natural state of being. Only in the last century has common law been methodically exchanged for civil law. Common law in its purest sense is an attempt to preserve rights: promote self-responsibility and personal growth; and express universal law on Earth.

Sovereignty: Sovereignty is the state of being people achieve when they have taken total self-responsibility for their lives and actions and for how these choices affect those around them.

Review what is happening all over the world. There are contradictions everywhere between philosophies espoused and actions taken. These contradictions are creating tremendous dysfunction on your world and send a confusing message to Earth's people. If you look closely, you will see that even though you are proclaiming a desire for spiritual and emotional sovereignty, you are actually perpetuating its opposite. This is causing a growing discontent within the hearts and minds of conscientious individuals.

Let us examine how deep is this sense of cultural non-sovereignty and how ancient this state of being truly is. Many people feel that educational, political or religious institutions are some of the cornerstones of physical existence. As an example, many individuals speak very highly of the Constitution of the United States and how it guarantees freedom for all people. Yet events have happened since 1776 that have very gradually deceived the people into believing they are on a path of freedom when in fact just the opposite is occurring.

Many of the belief systems set up on Earth were originally taught to you by your extraterrestrial forefathers thousands of years ago. Your forefathers were grappling with these same issues, and they looked to the Earth as a place where these issues could be healed once and for all. Now is a period in which people can either enslave themselves further or finally achieve sovereignty. Within the next fifty years people will need to make some decisions about planetary sovereignty and work together to achieve it.

There are many hidden compromises today that keep people enslaved. Here is an illustration. Society has told you that marriage is the only socially and legally sanctioned institution of romantic partnership. If you operate within the parameters of marriage, then you are led to believe that you have certain privileges not given to those without the license. These "privileges" might in fact be granted in exchange for the surrendering of your natural rights.

When you enter into a contract (such as for marriage) there are other issues at stake besides the idea of marriage. When you sign anything that has to do with a governing body, you will often relinquish certain rights. It is not very well known, but when you sign a marriage contract in some states of the U.S. you give up your right to educate your children the way you see fit or to choose your own preferred methods of health care or spiritual upbringing. Children become, in a sense, wards of the state. Depending upon the laws at any given time, then, the state ultimately controls the raising of your children. Though this might work well for parents who do not wish to be responsible for rearing their child, it is disempowering to the parents who wish to be responsible for themselves and their family. Where do *you* draw the line? Do you wish to surrender your human (and constitutional) rights in exchange for becoming dependent on an authoritarian state?

It is important to remember that someone is not necessarily out there deliberately trying to disempower you, but that because of your deep-seated emotional beliefs that have been perpetuated over thousands of years, society has created covert ways to keep itself disempowered. This might not be a case of someone stealing your power, but more a case of your freely giving it away. When power is freely given to a governing body, it snowballs, gathering more and more power and momentum as it rolls down the hill, incorporating everything in its path.

Originally, governments were meant only to serve and protect. The American separation from England was originally meant to free conscientious individuals from a tyrannical authoritarian body out of control. The desire was to create a self-responsible nation of sovereign beings. Has America now instituted a cycle of dependency, power struggles, and inequality?

At present you are not taught in school that you have a choice to keep or give away your natural power and sovereignty. The forefathers of the United States of America knew this and tried to instill it through the Constitution and the Bill of Rights. This handful of men known as the Founding Fathers had a strong spiritual background and wanted above all else to form a community based upon spiritual law. They were one of the first groups of humans after the fall of Atlantis to attempt the creation of a 4D model on Earth. They sensed the planetary energy changing and were ahead of their time. Their intentions were pure. However, as the snowball began to roll, the governing bodies began to convince the people that they needed protection from faceless enemies.

This protective entity evolved into the military complex, which must ensure its own survival. It also evolved into the senators and congressional representatives who profess to protect your interests but often serve only their own. It also evolved into tax collectors who operate unlawfully under the Constitution. It evolved into shadow government groups who operate outside of any law, and who sustain a bloated budget for black projects not approved by America's people or even Congress. Probably worst of all, it evolved into a self-preserving band of spin controllers who must at all costs manipulate public opinion in order to keep you asleep so they can perpetuate their agenda.

Becoming Responsible

All of this has happened because you gave away your power to choose your own destiny. You have become dependents instead of self-responsible sovereign beings. Even this, however, is all part of the greater plan. From this state of disempowerment you will truly learn about your own sovereignty.

When you relinquish your power to another person or institution, you have given up your sovereignty. Civil law ensures that someone is *always* a victim. It is built on the position that one party only is responsible for some act involving others. This predominant system reinforces the idea that, of two litigants, only one is at fault. If someone else is always to blame (of course each person takes for granted his own innocence), there must be a system in place to punish the "guilty." Thus, the perpetuation of victimhood continues with the sleight-of-hand that forces you to label yourself or others either guilty or innocent.

How often do you see an insurance commercial on television, where the insured person says, "It wasn't my fault. Don't I deserve something for my pain and suffering?" *This system rewards victims!* If this is true, does society really *want* to release the idea of victimhood? When you are a victim, you need not become responsible for yourself. This is attractive to many people.

Human beings never like overnight changes. It is too much of a shock. However, the majority of people are not aware they are perpetuating the cycle of fear, nonresponsibility, blame and victimhood. Imagine what it would be like if you were driving on the roads, and each and every person *knew* that they create their reality. What would happen if everyone knew that everything that happens to them was created by them for a very specific reason? Would they own their realities? Would they become more responsible?

If you believe you create your reality and you hit someone on the road, you would own it, take responsibility for it. Even if you were hit from behind, for instance, you would recognize that it is within your reality because you have somehow drawn it to you, for learning and growth. Once you release victimhood, you truly begin to support each other. You become a planetary community. Eventually you find that the rewards of self-responsibility far surpass the rewards you once received as a victim.

Imagine the structure of a society that held such beliefs. It would be a society that had no victims. It would be a society totally willing to take responsibility for everything that happened to its people. Humans are now working toward this, but because you have not identified the trap you have set for yourself, it is almost as if you are running on a treadmill. Once you recognize the depth of the structure your society has created, you will be able to begin actively changing it.

Some people have already begun doing this. However, some of the things you are trying to change are dragging you deeper into the mire. Let us say that a man studies the Constitution and recognizes the contradiction between what was intended and what is happening now. This person is used to the idea of "us" as victims and "them" as perpetrators. He becomes angry. Because he is not willing to look at the source of his anger—his addiction to victimhood and the probably inadvertent relinquishment of his sovereignty—he projects this onto the system. He decides to buck the system.

Let's say this man refuses to get automobile insurance, registration and a driving license. He intends to make an angry statement to cause trouble. This method will only create resistance, and will engage the very structure from which he is struggling to pull away. This will not free him from the structure, but keep him chained to it. Even though his actions might be justified, he has never looked at the real reason for his anger—the loss of his personal sovereignty. He instead blames the situation on someone else. You can never be sovereign if you *ever* blame anyone else.

Let us clarify the above statement. Withholding blame from another person does not mean blaming yourself instead. There should be no blame placed on anyone. When people engage in their own healing, they begin to embrace the idea that they create their own reality. However, they often misinterpret the idea and continue to place blame. The blame just shifts to the self. This is not freeing, it keeps you enslaved. Making this shift means relinquishing the whole idea of blame no matter *who* the target is. Focus instead on the self as the creator of reality for your own growth and learning. Learn the lessons, but never blame the self!

There are many individuals who feel they are doing good deeds because they are acting with anger against an unjust system. But anger will never solve the structural challenges of society. It will never break the structure, only perpetuate it. What, then, will break the structure? An intelligent understanding of the structure is a good place to start, as well as why and how the structure is kept in place. It becomes necessary to process all personal anger, martyrdom or victimhood that you feel in your life. Be honest with yourself and deal with the areas in your life where you feel powerless. You then must be willing to act from your own integrity rather than from anger or fear. Follow your conscience. Self-knowledge is freedom, because it allows you to be in touch with your motivations for action.

Humans are beginning to hear the clear voice of their conscience (rather than their anger) and process their emotional victimhood. They are beginning to understand the nature of the structure they want to change. As they realize in their own good conscience that they have a responsibility to change a weak or faulty structure, they must follow their own integrity.

In that choice to follow integrity cleanly, clearly and with no anger or blame, the structure begins to change. The issue is not that the structure itself enslaves you, but that you have *allowed* it to enslave you. If you can begin to understand the emotional reasons why your society has allowed the structure to be one of enslavement and why you have forgotten it was put there in the first place, true sovereignty is right around the corner. After that you will be able to see the still bigger picture and the beauty of the entire scenario created by all.

Fear and Sovereignty

If you create your reality, then it means that *everything* that happens is your creation—including being robbed, believe it or not! Many people place a lot of value on a lock, which after all is only a tiny piece of metal. Does this mean that if you want to process your fears, you should always leave your door unlocked? No. You must first process the internal energy before you act in the physical. It is *always* the internal that creates the external. If you do not process the internal, the external actions will not have the desired results and you might find yourself being victimized yet again.

If you process the fear first, one day there will be a welling of emotion, a feeling, or a shift in which the realization will come that you do not need to lock the doors anymore. That transformation cannot occur in the same way if you attempt to change the external before the internal has shifted.

Recognize that human beings are adept at transferring issues. If humans suddenly begin leaving their doors unlocked, they would manifest the unhealed fear of invasion in another area of their lives. If they try to eliminate the fear through mechanical means without processing it (such as by upgrading their security system), they will manifest the fear in another area. Fear will always be there in various forms until the internal dynamics are processed successfully.

As you go through your day-to-day life, try to notice every time you are not being totally responsible for your reality. Try to see where you fear being a victim. If you are very honest with yourself, you will see it very often during the day. Much of this is unconscious patterning. There are many individuals who put a lot of energy into the idea of victimhood. These individuals might have a difficult time with some of these concepts because it requires them to give up the familiar security of ever being a victim again.

You must recognize what you are doing when you reward yourself for pain, suffering or anything that is not of positive service to you. Insurance companies, for instance, will pay your medical bills *if* you are not to blame! This is a direct manifestation of the hidden and disempowering beliefs of your society. That concept is directly opposed to the higher ideals of common law and spiritual and emotional sovereignty. It is totally incompatible. To move easily into a 4D reality, one must cease the reinforcement of any disempowering behavior.

These disempowering structures are in place and people are struggling against them in an attempt to change them. However, you cannot see what you are struggling against. So the challenge now is to begin to see in the confused darkness the dim shapes of your own disempowered beliefs. These are the demons you have created to enslave yourselves. Layer by layer you will begin to relinquish these old structures, triggering enormously powerful changes. Sometimes you might think that you are at the end of the process only to find there are another five layers to go. You have been taught and then taught yourselves to believe that you need to be cared for, protected, and told what to do for your own good. The evolution of the species now demands that you enter adulthood and become a self-responsible species once and for all.

There is an intent to protect you from yourselves because it is assumed that you are not capable of doing it yourself. As an example, there are laws that force you to wear a helmet when you are driving a motorcycle. People allow this, even asking for more laws to control them! Fear will continue to be fed to you until you convince yourselves that you are nothing but powerless victims. The idea of keeping drugs illegal, for instance, is another false attempt to protect "innocent" people. How can you ever grow and evolve as a species if you are always being protected from the consequences of your actions?

The Founding Fathers

All of these systems endorsed by society stop you from understanding what sovereignty is. Sovereignty means taking total responsibility for yourself as an individual, for your community, and for your planet as a whole. This responsibility will not be learned through the imposition of laws, but through the genuine care and love of yourself and others.

There is a direct parallel between Masonry, America's Founding Fathers and the Sirian group of your extraterrestrial forefathers who attempted to liberate you in ancient days. In these ancient days there were two main extraterrestrial groups with genetic ties to you who were fighting for control of Earth. For simplicity, these two groups can be called the Lyrans (Lyra) and the Sirians (Sirius). In your ancient cultures they are identified by the symbols of the lion/cat (Lyra) and of the serpent (Sirius). For now, the information about these forefathers is highly generalized for the purposes of this illustration.

When the Sirian group attempted to liberate you from the Lyrans, they assumed that you needed help. Right there, a sense of inequality and victimization was being imposed upon you. Yet some of the Sirians' methods of protecting you are ones that the American Founding Fathers used as well. Some of these Sirian genetic engineers put specific genetic codes in you that were latent for a long time. These codes are beginning to fire in many of you now. It was a kind of insurance policy on the part of the Sirians to ensure that you would eventually be triggered into the awareness of your true heritage.

The American Founding Fathers did the same thing. They were very clever: It is not visible on the surface, but the way the Constitution is written is very specific and multi-dimensional. If it collapses due to the nefarious activities of various power structures or is perverted in any way, it will eventually turn around and work for your sovereignty instead of against it.

This is beginning to be visible today. The tighter the noose gets around the neck of the American population, the louder they cry, "Freedom!" The spiritual intentions of the Constitution (which were an attempt at physicalizing the 4D principles) are encoded within the cells of every person choosing to incarnate as an American. If there is an attempt to destroy these principles through shadow-government activity, the pressure will be felt deeply on a cellular level by all Americans, who will then in turn act out against the darkness. Each country in the world has a unique contribution to the transformation of Earth, and this is the particular service of America in this time.

The more oppressive your structure becomes, the more pressure individuals will feel. This will encourage people to do their own research. In doing so, they will learn about their rights (not their privileges) and begin exercising them. Freedom will not come by rejecting or fighting against privileges; it will come by *exercising rights.* Ultimately, you cannot use a negative force for a positive result.

The Founding Fathers were very shrewd. They knew that should anything in the Constitution be perverted, it would eventually work for sovereignty rather than against it. They did not necessarily understand what they were doing consciously. It was a knowingness, and they had much unseen guidance. They firmly believed in what they were doing.

You learned your current behavior from your extraterrestrial forefathers, who did not then have very enlightened ways of dealing with their challenges. You learned from them, for example, that the strongest one rules. You learned that someone has to be a victim and someone has to be an aggressor. Even to this day in the collective human soul, there is a belief that you do not own this planet. This was instilled in you eons ago. This belief is what has delayed you for so long in taking a global stand environmentally and socially.

You still do not believe that you exist and cocreate with the planet on equal terms, and you have no concept of your own sovereignty. In an attempt to feel sovereign, you typically take from others. All of the chaos in the world is an attempt to learn what true sovereignty is. Sooner or later the lesson will be learned. Reincarnationally speaking, many people on Earth now are incarnations of these extraterrestrial forefathers who are *still* trying to learn this lesson!

Advanced and evolved extraterrestrial civilizations believe in a set of unspoken principles. There are sovereign and nonsovereign planetary civilizations. Nonsovereign species are immature and often need protection—though *not* interference—because they do not recognize themselves as part of something vast and beautiful. They do not understand their own power. The way that extraterrestrial races interact with a planetary culture is based on the planet's sense of self-sovereignty. Extraterrestrial races are faced with the challenge of honoring a planet's state of nonsovereignty by not interfering in the planet's natural evolution, even if the planet is heading toward self-destruction. On the other hand, on sovereign planets there is a natural kinship between species meeting for the first time. There is never any aggression or an attempt to dominate. There is no hierarchy. But there is always hierarchy in a nonsovereign atmosphere because the planet's people do not know how to view reality in any other way.

As a species you have the right to interact with your galactic neighborhood. As a species you also have the right to know your heritage and to explore all levels of consciousness and reality. The universal rights mentioned above are always active. However, if you are not sovereign, you cannot interface with them. It is now time for the people of Earth to make an evolutionary leap.

This leap might seem too overwhelming to comprehend, so begin in a small way by focusing on the self. As each human evolves one by one, the whole becomes more than the sum of its parts. It is up to you.

16

OPENING THE HEART

The doorway into fourth density is through the heart. Only upon that path can you reunify all aspects of the self. To integrate the self, one must learn to love all aspects of creation, including the darkness within. To walk this path requires the courage to look into the mirror of the self. It also means allowing oneself to be vulnerable to the eyes and hearts of others. You must allow your true self to be revealed, because only then can you know yourself.

In many spiritual texts it has been discussed that opening the heart is a key ingredient of emotional and spiritual evolution. Though this is indeed accurate, the concept of opening the heart can at times seem vague and not easily applied in everyday life.

It is important to understand that an open heart cannot be achieved through the mind or the human will. In society today you have all become accustomed to taking action through the intellect only. Opening the heart is less a state of *doing* than it is of *being*. A mentally created reality is devoid of true emotional content and must rely upon mind, not emotion, for its survival. Thus humans often convince themselves that their relationships have emotional content when in fact the substance is simply a mentally created fantasy. Learning to generate reality and experience through the heart will change all aspects of life, including human relationships. When a reality is created by the mind, it leaves you searching for love and intimacy to complete it. When a reality is created by the heart, love and intimacy are an inherent component.

One cannot consciously create a state of being using the mind alone. However, one can put the self into an environment in which opening the heart becomes an essential key for maintaining that desired environment. In doing so, the conscious mind is surrendered and deeper processes within the self navigate you through the experience.

Here is a very simple exercise that will assist you to open the heart. It is an experiential exercise and cannot be done using the mind alone. The exercise is separated into three phases. You do not have to master all three. However, the three phases are presented for those who wish to take this teaching into the deepest levels of their life. The principles of each exercise are explained after the instructions.

OPENING THE HEART
(Exercise)

Phase One: Connecting with Beauty: Choose a quiet space and seat yourself comfortably. You will need a partner for this exercise. It is suggested that you use either a houseplant (the easiest) or a crystal. (A pet or any life form in motion would not be suitable because it would be distracting.) Begin to gaze at your "partner" with your open eyes.

It is important to breathe deeply and rhythmically. Deliberately seek the beauty in this partner. When you find beauty, hold that feeling. Your heart has begun to open. Find even more beauty. Once you learn to find beauty, you have the ability to always see more. When this exercise is practiced often, you will achieve the ability to open your heart quickly and learn the feeling of universal unconditional love.

✧ ✧ ✧

All humans have the capacity to appreciate beauty. In fact, it is a natural part of who you are. This ability keeps you connected to a universe that is seemingly comprised of chaos. When you deprive yourself of experiencing beauty, the heart begins to shut down. Then you begin to forget your origins and become distracted by 3D illusion. When you consciously seek the beauty in all things, the heart begins to open.

One does not need the mind to appreciate beauty. The mind does not feel threatened by the soul's need to appreciate the beauty in a sunset, nor does it need to understand the mechanics of why something is beautiful. The appreciation of beauty is one of the few instances in which the ego allows a transcendental experience to occur without interference. Your ability to perceive and appreciate beauty is the thread that keeps you connected to God.

The appreciation of beauty is simple. It does not require seminars to teach it to you. Even infants have this ability. You can see it in their faces as they gaze at a shiny object or at a spinning toy. This is why taking the time to appreciate beauty is an essential element in spiritual evolution. This appreciation of beauty nourishes your soul. It also teaches you to appreciate the beauty within yourself, since everything you gaze upon is ultimately a reflection of who you are.

In taking the time to appreciate the beauty of your plant partner, you are taking time to open your heart. Appreciating beauty and feeling love are synonymous. By practicing with your plant partner, you allow your heart to open without the pressure of thinking, "I must open my heart now." This process will bypass your mind and your inner critic. It can only be experiential.

By continuing this practice—and extending it into your everyday life with other forms of beauty you encounter or by continually seeking beauty—you can actually achieve states of ecstasy that increase in intensity. This initiates the phase-one healing process that begins to heal old wounds through the experience of profound love. The entire experience need never be judged or dissected for transformation within the self to take place.

By seeking beauty in order to open the heart, you make a conscious choice to live within a certain frequency. Be aware that stepping outside of that frequency of love and beauty is also a conscious choice. Through your choices and perceptions you can choose a third-density reality of separation or, using the lessons of third density, further your spiritual evolution. This does not mean that you must ignore the realities of 3D. It simply means that you must now choose the foundation upon which you live your life.

Phase Two: Finding Beauty within Another and within the Self: Phase two will require you to choose a human partner. It must be a person with whom you are willing to work deeply and intimately on an emotional level. Seat yourselves face to face in a comfortable position. Begin to look into each other's eyes and breathe deeply and rhythmically. Seek something of beauty within that person, a physical or a personality characteristic.

Appreciate that aspect of beauty. As you do this you will feel a swelling of emotion. Do not stop it. Find more aspects of beauty within that person. Keep breathing. Go deeper. Let your emotions rise to the surface. At some point in this exercise you might begin to feel fear, discomfort, shame, self-judgment, self-consciousness, guilt, or worthlessness. If these emotions occur, it is essential that you keep breathing deeply and appreciating the beauty of the other person.

✧   ✧   ✧

If you stop the exercise because of your uncomfortable emotions, you will close your heart. If you continue to breathe through these uncomfortable emotions and keep focusing on the beauty within the other person, you will eventually release a layer of negative emotion and experience a profound emotional healing. Also, it is important that you hold a safe space for your partner, who will also be experiencing these challenging and undesirable emotions. The more you engage in this exercise and move through the emotional blocks, the more layers of old emotional wounds will be released and healed.

This is an extremely powerful exercise and is often difficult to achieve successfully due to human insecurities. However, if emotional and spiritual healing and evolution are important to you, then you have all the inner resources necessary to see it through. If you continue to focus on the beauty of the other person while breathing and do not shut off the uncomfortable emotions, they will eventually release.

This exercise puts you in an extremely vulnerable state that cannot be controlled by the mind. If you continue to focus on the beauty and the breathing, you can work through a number of emotional blocks without ever understanding their origins. Remember, you never need to understand your emotions to heal them. This has been a common fallacy within many self-help programs. However, you must be willing to go deeply within the beauty and allow yourself to be vulnerable. If you do this, the natural healing processes of the self will navigate you through the experience successfully.

There is another byproduct of this exercise. By appreciating the beauty of another, you vicariously begin to appreciate the beauty within yourself. For many it has been too threatening and selfish to see beauty within the self, so the personality has created roadblocks toward self-appreciation. In learning to appreciate beauty within another, however, you automatically generate the energy of self-appreciation because the greater self knows that all life is connected to the same source. This deeper self understands that to give love and appreciate beauty in another is to see it within the self. In this way you fool the ego into accepting love and appreciation. Over time the ego no longer rejects it. Healing then becomes a natural and accepted part of the human experience.

You must use a human partner for this aspect of the exercise because one of the greatest fears of humans is to be naked, revealed, and vulnerable in the eyes of another. In doing this exercise you confront one of these great human fears, but you do so in a way that is as nonthreatening as possible. By confronting such a powerful and primal fear, one harnesses a great capacity for transformation. By doing so from a place of love and beauty, the fear rapidly transforms itself into a wealth of self-knowledge and rapid healing.

Phase Three: Heightening Intimacy: This exercise is similar to the teachings of tantra. It requires that you choose a partner with whom you are both sexually and emotionally intimate. Sexual intimacy without emotional intimacy will not fulfill the requirements of this phase. Seat yourselves comfortably and complete phase two as described above. When appropriate, begin engaging in intercourse in a face-to-face position, preferably while seated upright. The focus of this exercise is not in achieving pleasure through intercourse, but in heightening intimacy. Therefore, movement should be kept to a minimum. Gaze into each other's eyes and breathe deeply. Begin to find the beauty in your partner. Let that beauty open your heart. Keep breathing and travel deep into the eyes of your partner, seeking beauty at each new depth. With each breath inward, pull energy from the base of your spine up through your chakras. As you exhale, release love to your partner through the heart.

☼   ☼   ☼

This exercise is a multidimensional one because the exchange of love and emotional intimacy through sexuality has the capacity to free one's spirit from the confines of time and space. While doing this exercise you might have the sensation of approaching a door or barrier. If you keep breathing deeply, gazing at your partner and pulling the energy up the spine, you will eventually pass through that doorway. When you pass through, many new experiences and insights will reveal themselves to you. You might access past lives. (Most likely they will be those in which you have shared love with your partner.) You might feel a sense of traveling through the cosmos. You might also receive messages and wisdom from other realms. It is very common to receive profound insight into the self during these moments of extreme vulnerability.

There is one caution with this exercise. It is not to be treated lightly. If there are imbalances, power struggles, or unresolved issues in your relationship with your partner or if there is any mistrust, deceit, or insecurity, these emotions will be magnified tenfold during this exercise. If there are secrets being held in the relationship, they will be revealed.

You must enter this exercise with the awareness that it is for the purpose of expanding intimacy and the sacred marriage of the inner and outer male and female aspects. This exercise will not fix an ailing relationship. In fact, many couples have found that this type of intense intimacy has torn apart relationships that were based on unhealthy foundations. It is only for pioneering couples whose personal growth is more important than holding together a failing relationship. This exercise will either bring you infinitely closer or tear you apart.

All of the exercises suggested above are for the purpose of opening the heart and letting this heart energy begin to permeate your life. However, humans cannot truly open their hearts to others or to the world if they cannot forgive and love themselves. These exercises help to make the self-love process easier. However, as stated above, there might be a time when emotional toxins are released before the ecstasy is achieved. If this happens, do not be discouraged. It is part of the healing process. Continue forward. Eventually you will experience a profound sense of intimacy—not just with your partner, but with the universe and ultimately with yourself.

The New World Is Full of Love

You see yourselves as struggling to hold this planet together. You see yourselves as struggling with your everyday lives. What is really happening is something very different.

Humans are like beautiful butterflies whose heads are barely sticking out of their cocoons. As the planet moves further into fourth density, each butterfly might feel somewhat confused because it is in a new body. It will suddenly see a new world! It will have to learn the rules of the new world because the rules of the old one will no longer apply.

Do not think that the confusion you feel means that you are doing something wrong. Every time you feel that confusion, hold to your heart the image of the beautiful butterfly.

The new reality, symbolized by the new millennium, must now embrace conscious living. It contains joy and tears and togetherness. However, you can never truly be together until you become whole as individuals.

Don't forget to stretch your wings. When you do, you will discover that you really *can* fly!

ABOUT THE AUTHOR

Lyssa Royal is an internationally recognized author, lecturer and channel living in Phoenix, Arizona. While studying for her B.A. degree in Psychology, she developed an interest in hypnosis and learned to place herself in an altered state of consciousness for the purpose of stress management. In the early 1980s Lyssa had a dream in which a spiritual entity appeared and told her that she would "be a channel." Her self-hypnosis abilities helped her develop the necessary skills for her later development as a channel.

In 1979 Lyssa and her family witnessed an extraordinary UFO sighting near their family home in New Hampshire. This experience triggered an acute interest in extraterrestrial phenomena that propelled her into an in-depth study of the nature of human and extraterrestrial consciousness through her channeling and intuitive abilities. Though she works frequently with extraterrestrial information, the practical application of what she teaches and channels is her highest priority.

Lyssa Royal has been using her channeling skills professionally since 1985 by channeling for thousands around the world. She has frequently appeared on national and international television and on radio shows and is a regular contributor to magazines such as *The Sedona Journal of Emergence*. Lyssa has conducted extensive seminar tours throughout the USA, Japan, South Africa, Germany, and Australia and continues to lead tour groups to such ancient power spots as the Yucatan, England, Egypt, Peru, and Easter Island. Lyssa is the author of several books published in seven languages: *Millennium: Tools for the Coming Changes, Preparing for Contact, Visitors from Within,* and *The Prism of Lyra: An Exploration of Human Galactic Heritage.* Lyssa is listed in *Who's Who in American Writers, Editors, and Poets.*

Lyssa lives in Arizona with her husband Ron Holt and continues to write and travel worldwide. For more information send two stamps to:

Royal Priest Research
PO Box 30973
Phoenix, Arizona 85046
www.concentric.net/~lyra1/homepage.htm

206

MILLENNIUM MEDITATIONS
On Audio Tape
by
Lyssa Royal

Several key meditations suggested in *Millennium: Tools for the Coming Changes* have been recorded by Lyssa Royal and are available to be used a guided meditation tool to assist you in practicing the techniques discussed in the book.

<u>INCLUDED:</u>

Creating the Space for Abundance
Integrating the Inner Male and Female
Processing Darkness
Facing Fear
And More

To Order: Send check or money order for $14 to Royal Priest Research, PO Box 30973, Phoenix, Arizona 85046. Postage and handling is included. (Foreign orders, please add $3 per tape. U.S. Dollars Only). *Sorry, no credit cards.*

For a Complete Catalog and Schedule of Public Events
<u>Send Two Stamps to:</u>
Royal Priest Research
PO Box 30973
Phoenix, Arizona 85046

Royal Priest Research Internet Homepage:
http://www.concentric.net/~lyss/homepage.htm

Royal Priest Research Press
www.lyssaroyal.com
info@lyssaroyal.com

Books from Royal Priest Research

MILLENNIUM:
Tools for the Coming Changes
by Lyssa Royal

Since the mid-1980s Lyssa Royal has been receiving groundbreaking information and teachings from the spiritual realms. For the first time ever, some of the most profound teachings that have been given through Lyssa are synthesized into book form.

Millennium intimately explores the global shift in consciousness, the inner workings of the human psyche and the nature of reality in a way that inspires readers to bring more happiness, fulfillment, and self-empowerment into their lives. *Millennium* offers instruction to those readers who wish to incorporate the teachings into their lives through simple yet effective techniques designed to shift the perception of the reader and thus their very reality itself. *Millennium* is an effective guidebook to navigate the uncharted waters of the new millennium with ease, grace, self-confidence, and an open heart.

ISBN 0-9631320-3-2, $13.95   **New!**

PREPARING FOR CONTACT
A Metamorphosis of Consciousness
by Lyssa Royal and Keith Priest

This groundbreaking book is a combination of narrative, precisely focused channeled material and personal accounts. An inside look at the ET contact experience is given including what the human consciousness experiences during contact with an extraterrestrial and how our perceptions of reality change during contact. The authors present a breathtaking look at the contact phenomenon and its connection to the evolution of the human race.

ISBN 0-9631320-2-4, $12.95   Japanese/German/Polish

VISITORS FROM WITHIN
by Lyssa Royal and Keith Priest

This book explores the extraterrestrial contact and abduction phenomenon in a unique and intriguing way. A combination of narrative, precisely focused channeled material and first-hand accounts, this book challenges the reader to use the abduction phenomenon as a tool for personal and planetary evolution. It will encourage you to expand your beliefs about extraterrestrial contact forever.

ISBN 0-9631320-1-6, $12.95   Japanese/German/Korean/Polish

THE PRISM OF LYRA
An Exploration of Human Galactic Heritage
by Lyssa Royal and Keith Priest

This introductory book examines the idea of creation in a different light. In contrast to the notion that humans are the result of creation, it explores the idea that the collective humanoid consciousness (or soul) created our universe for specific purposes. *The Prism of Lyra* then traces various developing off-planet races (such as cultures from Lyra, Sirius, Orion and the Pleiades) through their own evolution and ties them into the evolving Earth. Highlighted is the realization of our galactic interconnectedness and our shared desire to return home.

ISBN 0-9631320-0-8, $11.95 Japanese/German/Korean/Polish/Chinese/Portuguese

To Order: You may order any of the above books in the english language from your local bookstore or by sending a check or money order to Royal Priest Research, PO Box 30973, Phoenix, Arizona 85046. Please add $3.00 shipping for the first book and $1.50 for each additional book. Foreign orders, please add $5. U.S. dollars only. *Sorry, we do not accept credit card orders.*